Claude Duneton, *Chroniqueur* at *Le Figaro*

Claude Duneton, *Chroniqueur* at *Le Figaro*

By

Mary Munro-Hill

Cambridge Scholars Publishing

Claude Duneton, *Chroniqueur* at *Le Figaro*

By Mary Munro-Hill

This book first published 2018

Cambridge Scholars Publishing

Lady Stephenson Library, Newcastle upon Tyne, NE6 2PA, UK

British Library Cataloguing in Publication Data
A catalogue record for this book is available from the British Library

ISBN (10): 1-5275-0769-6
ISBN (13): 978-1-5275-0769-2

I DEDICATE THIS BOOK TO MY HUSBAND, THOMAS PETER HILL,
MY PARENTS, JOHN AND JOAN MUNRO,
AND MY LIFELONG FRIENDS, MARGUERITE CANEL,
JEAN AND THÉRÈSE GUILHEM,
AND MICHÈLE GAY.

CLAUDE DUNETON AND MARY MUNRO-HILL
RUE DE DUNKERQUE, PARIS, JULY 1994
TAKEN BY THOMAS PETER HILL © MARY MUNRO-HILL

TABLE OF CONTENTS

LIST OF ILLUSTRATIONS

PREFACE

CLAUDE DUNETON,
CHRONIQUEUR AT *LE FIGARO*

It was in July 1994 that I first had the pleasure of meeting Claude Duneton. We had been corresponding for some months following the completion of my doctoral thesis on Aristide (Maurice Chapelan), in which he had shown particular interest, since he was at the time seriously considering a proposal from *Le Figaro* that he should become *chroniqueur du langage* at the newspaper, writing a weekly language article for its literary supplement.

Duneton had in fact already started to contribute a regular *rubrique langagière* for *Le Figaro littéraire* in April of that year, though only on a temporary basis, since he was asking himself, as a man of distinctly anti-establishment leanings, who had been—and was still—a fervent communist and *soixante-huitard*, whether he could in all conscience work for a right-wing publication, with whose politics he could not possibly sympathise. We discussed this ethical question at some length at our first meeting, during which I assured him that Maurice Chapelan, in all his forty-odd years as *critique littéraire* and then as resident *chroniqueur du langage* at *Le Figaro* from April 1961 to his death in March 1992, had never once felt obliged to express or defend any political opinion in his writing.

After careful consideration Claude subsequently signed a contract with *Le Figaro* and became the newspaper's resident grammarian, Aristide's successor, until his work was cruelly curtailed in 2010 by a disabling stroke.

Following our initial meeting, when I had given Claude a copy of my PhD thesis, he honoured both Aristide and me on 4 November 1994 in a charming and sensitive *chronique*, entitled *Cher Aristide*, the closing paragraph of which I am pleased to reproduce here:

> *L'auteur britannique avoue avoir voulu « servir à immortaliser* Aristide *of* Le Figaro *». Belle fidélité de la part de Mrs Munro [sic], correspondante et lectrice assidue de Maurice Chapelan, qu'elle connaissait en personne, et qui la cita plusieurs fois dans ses chroniques. En ces journées de*

remembrance et d'affectueux salut, auquel je m'associe, il y a de la
douceur, cher Aristide, dans cet épais volume érudit : c'est le plus beau
des chrysanthèmes !

My husband Peter and I visited Claude in his vast apartment in the rue
de Compiègne, not far from the Gare du Nord, where I immediately felt at
home, as there were books and papers strewn everywhere. His desk was
overflowing and the floor was littered with documents. There was
evidence of much work in progress: indeed, Claude was at the time putting
the finishing touches to the second part of his *magnum opus* on the history
of French song, *Histoire de la chanson française,* the magnificent result of
many years of exhaustive research, eventually published in 1998 in two
volumes by the Éditions du Seuil.

Claude had been—and still was—an admirer of *le grand écrivain*
Alexandre Vialatte, who for twenty years had written a weekly *chronique*
for *La Montagne.* Vialatte had invariably closed his articles with the
words: « Et c'est ainsi qu'Allah est grand », a custom imitated from time to
time by Duneton, who offered his interpretation of those ritualistic words
in his article *Allah et Alex* on 14 January 2010: « C'est ainsi que les choses
adviennent, nous n'y pouvons rien », a vague expression of fatalism and
resignation. He adds:

Il m'est donc arrivé, au cours de ces dernières années, de terminer un
article par cette chute fameuse, par respect pour le grand chroniqueur
mort (en 1971).

He was undeterred by the misplaced recriminations of some of his
readers—who, incidentally, were not Muslims, Christians or Jews—who
accused him of taking the name of Allah in vain.

In his opinion, the greatest living *chroniqueur de langue française* was
Pierre Foglia, columnist at *La Presse*, Montréal. Duneton saw in Foglia a
worthy successor to Vialatte, whom he had held in the highest possible
esteem.

At first glance Claude Duneton and his immediate predecessor at *Le
Figaro,* Maurice Aristide Chapelan, could scarcely have been more
different from each other in background and temperament, yet they had
much in common: they both enthusiastically contributed weekly articles
on the French language for the same newspaper, Aristide for just over
thirty years and Claude for sixteen; both experienced success in the
literary world, each of them versatile and prolific writers in several genres
and both receiving prestigious prizes from *l'Académie française.* As well

as writing and translating, they had both been engaged in the world of theatre and cinema.

As a child in the early years of the twentieth century, Maurice Chapelan had been seriously ill with asthma, for which there were then none of the miracle-cures we know today; Claude Duneton, too, was seriously ill in childhood, an apparent misfortune at the time but one which would change the course of his life, since lengthy hospitalisation in Paris would give him a grounding in the French language. Explaining why he was linguistically different from the other six-year-old children starting school at Lagleygeolle in 1941, some of whom spoke nothing other than *l'occitan*, usually termed *patois*, Claude tells us (Duneton 1973: 11):

> *Parce qu'à deux ans une maladie grave m'avait valu un long séjour dans un hôpital à Paris. J'avais donc par hasard appris à parler français en premier lieu et mes parents avaient continué sur cette lancée.*

It is perhaps not surprising, in view of my earlier book, *Aristide of Le Figaro* (Cambridge Scholars Publishing, 2017), that I should wish to draw comparisons here and there, and point out differences, too, between the two French *chroniqueurs* I have known.. Aristide and his articles had evolved over the years, as one of his correspondents remarked (4 January 1985): « Il est vrai que vous avez gagné en humour ce que vous semblez avoir perdu en sévérité ». Whereas his earlier articles, appearing under the heading *Usage et grammaire*, had been scholarly and serious, his later contributions, bearing from early in 1986 the more appropriate title of *Divertissements grammaticaux*, were, although still scholarly, rather more light-hearted and entertaining. Indeed, of his own *chroniques,* even those of his earlier days at *Le Figaro*, Aristide wrote (Chapelan 1977: 61):

> *J'enfile volontiers la venelle sous le moindre prétexte langagier, et mes chroniques sont des flâneries qui m'amusent, avant d'amuser, du moins me l'écrivent-ils, la plupart de mes lecteurs. Ce délayage n'en contient pas moins, à chaque fois, l'élucidation d'un point de vocabulaire ou de syntaxe, qu'il rend ainsi plus agréable d'avaler. J'espère même que de la sorte l'efficacité en est plus grande.*

Duneton's *chroniques*, on the other hand, although certainly containing more than a trace of humour, were from the beginning academic and didactic, as befits a former schoolmaster, and remained so until the end, as we shall see. Unlike Aristide, Claude tended more often than not to adhere to one subject at a time, although he, too, occasionally enjoyed wandering off the point.

In my book on Aristide, I posed this question, among others: why are there now relatively few dedicated *chroniqueurs du langage* in the French press? I wondered at the time whether their gradual decline in number reflected a general loss of interest in correct usage or whether André Gide had been right in his opinion that Maurice Grevisse, with his seminal work on French grammar, *Le Bon Usage*, had rendered the *chroniqueurs du langage* redundant.

I have since concluded that the many French grammar pages to be found on the Internet—including the *Langue française* section of *Culture* in the electronic version of *Le Figaro,* a leader in the field, with its *forum*—have assumed the role of those writers who, like Claude Duneton and Maurice Aristide Chapelan before him, dealt with readers' linguistic uncertainties in their weekly columns, as they covered various aspects of the language.

Aristide may accordingly have been mistaken (9 January 1989) in his assumption that anyone like him, a newspaper-grammarian, would have a job for life, *ressemblant dans [mon] boulot aux médecins, aux pharmaciens et aux marchands d'armes... Aucun risque. Dieu merci !*

There may now be fewer weekly *chroniques du langage* in the French press, but a quick search on the Internet reveals the vast number of sites intended for native French speakers who are unsure of their grammar and wish to increase their understanding of the mechanics of the language in order to improve their linguistic skills, both spoken and written. It is clear that the desire to be reminded of forgotten rules of grammar is as strong now as ever it was, certainly among Internet users, *les internautes*, though the press in general has almost ceased employing resident weekly *chroniqueurs du langage*. In the case of the online edition of *Le Figaro* there is now a daily forum under the page *Langue française* in the *Culture* section, mentioned above, inviting readers to submit their queries. The forum is managed by several journalists. It is more than a little surprising to see the kind of very elementary questions posed by readers.

The World Wide Web seems to have taken the place not only of encyclopaedias but of all kinds of manuals covering almost every subject under the sun. It is possible to study the most arcane of matters—some free of charge—*en ligne*. As people all over the world are now able to read their newspapers on their laptops, tablets and smart-phones, it is only to be expected that printed papers and journals are gradually disappearing: *France-Soir* and *La Tribune* are available only *en version numérique*, just as *The Independent* in the United Kingdom is now a solely electronic publication. On the other hand, when *liseuses*, such as the famous *Kindle* and the less well-known *Nook* and *Kobo,* first came on the scene and rapidly gained thousands of customers, many people feared the imminent demise of the printed book, but, contrary to their anticipation, the latest statistics indicate that traditional printed books are now regaining their popularity and fewer people are using electronic readers.

Since Claude's death I have made a study of his *chroniques du langage*, all of which bear the entirely appropriate title *Le plaisir des mots*, clearly illustrating his passion for words above all other aspects of the French language. Although his articles deal occasionally with the same questions treated by Aristide and his *confrères*, Claude's emphasis is far more often on words and their history than on actual grammar.

As Aristide had done in 1989 with his *La langue française dans tous ses débats* (François Bourin), covering the period 1961 to 1988, Duneton published a collection of his articles, *Au plaisir des mots* (Balland, 2004), the second edition of which appeared as *Au plaisir des mots: les meilleures chroniques* (Denoël, 2005), encompassing the decade 1994 to 2004.

After Maurice Chapelan's death in March 1992 it was two years before a permanent grammarian was found to replace him. The well-known writer, Paul Guth, took over the column for a few months, calling his article *L'Art d'écrire*, but as his *chroniques* were concerned distinctly more with literature than with language *Le Figaro* did not engage him as Aristide's successor.

In April 1994 Claude took over the column, temporarily, as we have seen, and now, in 2018, six years after his death, *Le Figaro* is still reproducing his *chroniques* in its electronic paper, under the heading *Langue française*, with this comment:

> Retrouvez les chroniques de Claude Duneton (1935-2012) chaque semaine. Écrivain, comédien et grand défenseur de la langue française, il tenait avec gourmandise la rubrique *Le plaisir des mots* dans les pages du *Figaro littéraire*.

ACKNOWLEDGMENTS

First of all I acknowledge my deep debt of gratitude to the late Claude Duneton himself, not only for his willingness to meet me on several occasions but also for his hospitality and for his generosity in giving me copies of his books.

As well as expressing my gratitude to Claude, I must thank his daughter, Noémie, who in that same spirit of kindness has given me invaluable help, supplying biographical details and photographs of Claude, which I have used in this work.

My parents, too, I must thank, albeit belatedly, for the sacrifices they made when I was at school, and later at university, to enable me to make annual visits to France.

I am also greatly indebted to the staff of Cambridge Scholars Publishing, whose assistance has made the preparation of this book such a pleasure.

Introduction

Claude Duneton :
L'HOMME ET L'ŒUVRE

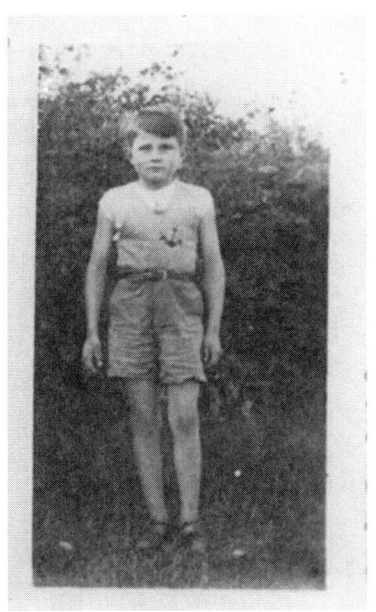

Claude Duneton was born in the village of Lagleygeolle (La Gleisòla in *occitan*) in Corrèze on Sunday 21 April—Easter Day—1935, into a peasant family. He had a hard childhood during the Occupation. His father had been severely affected by his experiences in the First World War at Verdun and had returned home in 1918 to discover that his wife had died of influenza in the pandemic. Claude's mother, therefore, was his father's second wife, much younger than he and a rather ill-tempered woman. In an interview with Thierry Gandillot of *L'Express*, published on 20 December 2004, Claude described his mother as « mauvaise avec tout le monde ».

His early life at school is vividly depicted in his best-known work, *Parler croquant* (Stock, 1973); *l'occitan* was spoken at home by all in Lagleygeolle, with the exception of Claude and both his parents, who had worked in Paris for a while and therefore spoke standard French. *L'occitan* was banned, however, from the class-room, and Claude's fellow-pupils were forced to lead a double life, speaking *une langue étrangère*, a truly foreign language, *le français*, in class, and their normal tongue, *la langue d'oc*, *l'occitan* or *le patois*, as they called it, outside school. Claude's own position was most unusual, in that he spoke French both at home and in class but *l'occitan* when in the company of his friends.

CLAUDE DUNETON IN 1948
© ARCHIVES FAMILLE DUNETON

Shortly before Claude suffered his stroke, he had engaged in a highly personal conversation with his good friend and fellow-author, Jacques Cassabois, in which he had spoken freely of his early life; I have been privileged to receive from Claude's daughter, Noémie, what is in effect a transcript of that exchange, as Jacques had carefully noted it all at the time.

On 23 March 2010, Claude and Jacques had returned to the Hôtel de Flandres in Compiègne, where Claude was appearing in a production of Raymond Depardon's *La ferme du Garet*. He and Jacques, who had come expressly to see the performance that evening, had retired for the night, quite weary after the play and the ensuing civic reception, but were both up and about before six o'clock the next morning, refreshed. As they waited for their breakfast they started to chat about wide-ranging matters and Claude suddenly introduced the topic of fate, *la destinée*, sharing with Jacques many details of how significant a role it had played in his early life. Since Jacques had noted it so accurately at the time, he was able to pass on to Claude's children the whole of that precious conversation, which he addressed simply to *Philippe, Olivier, Louise et Noémie* with this introduction:

> On s'intéresse rarement à l'enfance de ses parents, et puis, un jour, quand la curiosité nous vient, ils ne peuvent plus nous répondre…J'ai écrit ce texte à partir des notes, consignées immédiatement après une conversation avec Claude, en pensant à ses enfants, à qui je dédie ces lignes.

The conversation, so conscientiously recorded in writing by Jacques, more than adequately corroborates the less detailed interviews Claude had given previously, especially that granted to Thierry Gandillot in December 2004. Claude had recounted how he was sent by his father to be trained as a fitter at the *Centre d'Apprentissage* at Brive but his academic ability had soon become evident and his masters realised that such a clever boy was in the wrong place.

His attachment to his linguistic roots would remain with him throughout his life: he who had acquired a perfect mastery of French language and literature would always remember the *parler* of his *village natal* and would unceasingly champion *l'occitan* and all other regional and minority languages.

In his review of *Au plaisir des mots*, Thierry Gandillot of *L'Express* included an interview with Claude, conducted shortly after the publication of the first edition of his collection of *chroniques*. During that interview Claude had spoken of his lifelong passion for language and had answered many questions Thierry had posed, including why the French as a nation are so fascinated by their native tongue. The conversation had turned inevitably to Claude's childhood. He had reflected on his early linguistic experiences at Lagleygeolle, describing them as confusing and uncomfortable for him, as he had fallen between two stools: although surrounded by the familiar sounds of *l'occitan* he had spoken French (an alien language to the other children in his community, though not to him) both at home with his parents and, of course, at school. This initial confusion awakened in him a curiosity about language *per se* and would eventually develop into a love which would claim all his attention and dictate his path for the rest of his life. He explained to Gandillot the process involved in this evolution, remarking how all one's life one tries to answer the questions of childhood:

> *Ma curiosité vient de là. Toute sa vie, on tente de résoudre les questions qu'on s'est posées entre 2 et 5 ans. La fascination vient aussi de l'inquiétude face à une langue imposée par les élites.*

One wonders why Claude, who had been taken to Paris as a child of two, did not mention during the interview the significance of his long stays in hospital there, where he had first encountered standard French.

Despite a difficult start in life, acquainted with both poverty and illness, Claude would succeed in all he did. Having been made to leave school when his parents could no longer afford to keep him there, he eventually returned at the age of sixteen and was placed *en cinquième* with pupils three years younger.   He was very soon promoted to a more appropriate year and came top of the class before moving on to the prestigious Lycée Henri-IV in Paris, for which he received a grant, much to the relief of his father.   On paper, the Dunetons seemed quite well-off, as they owned land, but in reality they were very poor.

As he wished to become a teacher, Claude trained from 1952 to 1954 at the *École Normale* at Tulle, his main ambition in those days being to return to Lagleygeolle as a respected schoolmaster and to live in a house with running water, having had more than his fair share, he felt, of bucket-filling. In order to qualify as a secondary school teacher, Claude attended the *École Normale* at Clermont-Ferrand. His first post was at the *Collège* at Meyssac, five kilometres from Lagleygeolle. His teaching subject was English, which he loved.

In 1971 Duneton and his family (his first wife Germaine and their two sons) moved from Corrèze to the *région parisienne*. Claude was sent to Fontainebleau in 1971 and to Savigny-sur-Orge in 1972, where he remained as a *professeur d'anglais* until leaving the teaching profession.

According to his close friend, fellow-*Corrézien* and contemporary, Jean Meyssignac, who himself is a *chroniqueur* at *France-Catholique*, Claude's childhood was made all the more difficult by his serious illness, a dislocation of both hips, a condition that would affect not only his childhood but the rest of his life, as he would always walk with a limp and would never be able to take part in sports:

> Les Duneton étaient pauvres et Claude est né handicapé. [...] Mère et fils partirent à Paris pour des opérations et de longs séjours dans les hôpitaux. C'est là qu'il apprit à parler. C'est pourquoi ce pur sujet de la Vicomté de Turenne parlait avec un fond d'accent parisien.

Jean might have added at this point that it was not simply a slight Parisian accent that Claude had acquired but, more importantly, a familiarity with the standard French language, thanks to his long periods in hospital—the only possible advantage of his childhood illness.

As the condition had been overlooked at his birth, when it might have been treated in a relatively simple manner at home, it became necessary for him to make frequent visits to Paris for surgical treatment, starting in early childhood. The dysplasia had prevented Claude from learning to walk properly. His parents had noticed that he was waddling rather than walking and it was then that their family doctor had diagnosed the problem. Noémie tells me that despite undergoing several operations, both during his childhood and in later life, the condition had left him with permanent problems. As well as the many early operations, he underwent further surgery on his hips in 1968 and even as late as 1989. He also had a stent fitted in 1997, to relieve the cardiac problems which would, sad to relate, eventually return with greater severity.

Claude had married for the first time in the early 1960s and had his two sons by Germaine, who was also a teacher: Philippe in 1961 and Olivier in 1963. In 1987 Claude's daughter, Louise, was born, to be followed in 1990 by his youngest child, Noémie. The girls' mother, whom Claude married in 1990, is the writer, radio *réalisatrice*, journalist and magazine-editor, Isabelle Yhuel (who kept the name of her first husband). Although his two marriages ended in divorce, Claude remained on good terms with both Germaine and Isabelle.

Germaine and he separated around the time that Claude was embracing his writing career, when his life was changing dramatically. His preoccupation with his work had made him rather difficult to live with and led to tensions between the couple. As far as his separation from Isabelle was concerned, it was, conversely, her professional life that was evolving and unsettling Claude, who found the situation difficult to handle. Nevertheless, intimate relationships were important to him and he had other women in his life, of whom he remained fond, keeping in touch with them long after their relationships had ended. Claude was a kind and loving man, whose warmth, humour and sincerity were much appreciated by his friends and family.

Duneton was a gifted, prolific and passionate writer, but of all the many genres he mastered during his long career it was his weekly *chronique du langage* for *Le Figaro littéraire* that brought him the greatest pleasure and satisfaction, the work to which he was naturally most attached, since words were his true *métier* and his primary concern: *les mots*, their meaning, their use, their history, their etymology. The hundreds of *chroniques* he wrote for *Le Figaro* bear this out most eloquently.

His first foray into the world of the *rubrique langagière* in the press had in fact taken place many years earlier. Following the resounding success of his *Parler croquant* in 1973, he was invited by the magazine *Elle* to write a regular *chronique du langage*. This invitation he accepted with alacrity, and he happily wrote those language articles for four or five years. The experience would serve as an invaluable preparation for his sixteen years as resident *chroniqueur* at *Le Figaro littéraire*.

Claude was never more at home and never happier than when he was writing his *chroniques*. With an etymological dictionary in one hand and a pen in the other, surrounded by his many works of reference, Claude truly enjoyed his work. He took his linguistic writing seriously, researching it thoroughly and painstakingly, and he was so committed to his position as *chroniqueur* at *Le Figaro littéraire* that he always had a few articles ready in advance, « *pour le cas où…* ». The title of his articles, *Le plaisir des mots*, was perfectly fitting, since his study of words as *chroniqueur* brought him infinite joy and delight.

He told me on more than one occasion: *J'adore écrire dans les journaux*. In the preface to his collection of articles, *Au plaisir des mots* (2005: 11), he explains why he so enjoys writing his *chroniques*:

> *Le partage presque immédiat avec des lecteurs et des lectrices du contenu d'un article m'offre une compensation à l'effort solitaire de l'écriture « au long cours » qui est celle d'un livre. C'est comme entretenir une conversation, une causette imaginaire où j'ai le temps, cependant, de limer ma réplique ; moi qui, au naturel, ai l'esprit de l'escalier, je me donne là l'illusion de la vivacité !*

Many of his readers wrote to him, commenting on his articles, asking him questions and suggesting topics for him to treat, from which Claude frequently chose items to cover in his *chroniques*; in turn he wrote letters, sometimes to his English friends, asking for advice and seeking information. Some such letters he occasionally addressed to me, in response to which I recommended on one occasion Brewer's *Dictionary of Phrase and Fable* and on another *The Oxford Dictionary of Quotations*.

CLAUDE DUNETON CHRISTMAS 2009 © JEAN TIGÉ

Having left his apartment at 2 rue de Compiègne in 1999, Claude divided his time from the early 2000s between his house in Corrèze, originally that of his grandparents, and his pied-à-terre in Paris, *au XVe*. His life in Lagleygeolle, as both child and man, would lead to one of his most important works, *Le Monument* (Balland, 2010), « roman vrai », a true story.

In 2010 tragedy struck, when Claude suffered a debilitating stroke, a cruel blow, which brought his writing career to a premature end. He was in hospital in Lille when that terrible event took place. He had suffered a series of mini-strokes, transient ischaemic attacks, and was awaiting cardiac surgery, which he had opted to have performed in Lille, as his doctor son Olivier practised there and knew the surgeons concerned. When Claude had his stroke he was actually about to be discharged from the hospital for a few days, pending the scheduled surgery, so that he could organise his *Figaro littéraire* articles and have a few in hand ready for publication.

Noémie tells me that the stroke paralysed her father down his right-hand side and made it impossible for him to form words. However, he understood everything, and his family came gradually to understand him. Although communication was very difficult it was not completely absent, but Claude could no longer read and write, and this made life especially hard for him. He died in a residential home in Lille on 21 March 2012, one month short of his seventy-seventh birthday.

Many warm obituaries appeared in the press, among which was that of Jean-Claude Raspiengeas in *La Croix* on 22 March:

> L'écrivain truculent, l'acteur de composition, le philologue de la langue populaire est mort mercredi 21 mars à Lille, à 77 ans, loin de Lagleygeolle, son village de Corrèze. Il espérait que la mort viendrait le saisir chez lui, à Lagleygeolle, son village natal de Corrèze, « le plus tard possible ».

Le Figaro wrote, also on 22 March:

> Notre ami Claude Duneton s'est éteint mercredi 21 mars, à l'âge de 77 ans. Chroniqueur au *Figaro littéraire* depuis une dizaine d'années, sa rubrique *Au plaisir des mots* faisait la joie des lecteurs, qui ne manquaient pas de le lui dire chaque semaine.

Most of the obituaries made the same mistakes, stating his age at death as seventy-seven, when it was in fact seventy-six, and giving the title of his *chronique* as *Au plaisir des mots*, which was the title of his published collection of articles, the *chronique* itself being *Le plaisir des mots*. The latter was a surprising slip on the part of *Le Figaro*, the very publication for which Claude had written for sixteen years, although the reporter unfortunately reduced his time at the newspaper to *une dizaine d'années*. These mistakes are unfortunate and disappointing.

Claude himself had spoken movingly of his end, during an extended interview with Raspiengeas, which the journalist reproduced, in a much fuller obituary of Claude, in *La Croix* on 23 March 2012:

> Imaginant sa fin et son repos éternel à Lagleygeolle, en terre occitane, Claude Duneton avait exprimé un souhait : « Que quelqu'un sache encore me regretter d'une parole fraternelle : lou pauré téchou ! » Lou pauré téchou—the pauvre petit...

CHAPTER ONE

FIDÈLES LECTEURS

Ce qui me soutient c'est le courrier, les réactions généralement aimables,
serviables, d'un public cultivé qui me propose des réponses et m'apporte
quelquefois des précisions essentielles.
—Claude Duneton, *Au plaisir des mots : les meilleures chroniques,* Denoël,
2005, page 12.

All *chroniqueurs du langage* owe much to their readers for their valued
contributions to discussions, and Claude is no exception. He dedicates his
anthology *À mes fidèles lecteurs* and often mentions them by name. A reader
may sometimes challenge the stated opinion of the *chroniqueur,* as was the
case in September 2003, when Claude quoted from a letter he had received
from a correspondent, Marcel Guibert, from La Varenne-Saint-Hilaire, who
had served in the army during the Second World War and wished to provide
authentic and convincing information in the quarrel between those affirming
the expression *au temps pour moi*, deriving from military terminology, and
those supporting the phrase *autant pour moi*, the only acceptable form,
according to Claude.

The argument had begun many years earlier, in *Le Figaro littéraire* of 14
September 1995, when Claude had asserted that *au temps* was *la fausse
graphie*. In his collection of articles (2005: 15) he writes:

Ce qui est réjouissant dans une chronique de très longue durée c'est...le
radotage ! Je veux dire par là les sujets qui reviennent périodiquement, avec
la constance de l'idée fixe, particulièrement lorsqu'on a oublié avoir déjà
parlé de la chose.

Referring to the articles he had written on the subject since September 1995,
he commented, not without humour, on 18 December 2003, that at this rate
they ran the risk of creating two camps in France: *les « autantistes » et les*
« autempestifs ». He went on to say, making abundantly clear the fact that
he disagreed wholeheartedly with the grammarians quoted:

J'ai reçu de fiévreuses protestations à la suite de mes remarques sur l'erreur sémantique qui consiste à vouloir écrire « au temps pour moi » la locution autant pour moi ». On a brandi le Dictionnaire d'orthographe d'André Jouette, *on m'a menacé du* Grevisse *[...]*

On another matter—a further instance of *radotage*—far removed from the military context of the foregoing, though attracting equally belligerent arguments, Claude criticises (2005: 23) the false etymology, *aberration courante,* of the word *croque-mort.* The common misconception is that *le croque-mort*, the undertaker's assistant, was the person whose task it was to bite the big toe of a corpse in order to ensure that the deceased was well and truly dead before nailing down the lid of the coffin.

Claude has certainly dealt with this etymological misunderstanding before, for we read (2005: 127):

D'où vient notre croque-mort ? Le mot apparaît pour la première fois dans l'écrit en 1788. Or, à cette époque, le français familier connaît un autre sens de « croquer » que celui de « broyer avec les dents », un sens parallèle, sans doute issu du même étymon : « croc », qui est « voler, subtiliser, dérober », etc. Cette acception était déjà tout à fait bien établie au XVe siècle, comme le prouve ce passage des chroniques de Louis XI : « Il aperçut sur le bord de la cuve un très beau diamant qu'elle avait osté de son doigt : si le croqua si souplement qu'il ne fut d'âme aperçu » (in Littré).

Whether or not this paragraph casts any light on the meaning or derivation of *croque-mort* is debatable. Surely Claude does not wish us to see in this compound noun an allusion to body-snatching…

It should be pointed out that the two articles on the subject of *croque-mort* appear in the wrong order in the anthology, destroying the chronology. Returning to the subject, he refers obliquely to the eighteenth-century date previously mentioned:

On nage évidemment en plein délire—vous avez eu connaissance d'un métier pareil au XVIIIe siècle ? Cependant l'explication plaît par son apparence « rationnelle ». Le mot vient d'un vieux sens de croquer *qui est « frapper », comme dans « croque-note » ; le croque-mort est celui qui cloue le cercueil, et semble ainsi donner des coups au pauvre mort en partance. C'est une plaisanterie de corbillard !*

One senses here both Claude's final word on the subject and his amused incredulity as he writes, his light touch of humour being much in evidence. We note, too, that he supplies information about the verb *croquer* not provided in his earlier *chronique*, although, as he does not wish to shock his *fidèles lecteurs*, he refrains from speaking indelicately about the meaning of the verb provided in *Le Dictionnaire comique* of 1752 by Philibert Le Roux, who gives it the sense of « attraper, duper », with the following example borrowed from the Italian theatre:

> C'est que la plupart sont des goulus, qui ne veulent de femmes que pour eux : ils ont beau faire, on en *croquera* toujours quelques-unes à leur barbe.

He does not hesitate, however, to speak his mind bluntly here and there, at times with surprising candour, when finding erroneous the opinion of a colleague. In the case under discussion, the etymology of *croque-mort*, Claude tells how his fellow-*chroniqueur*, Jean-Pierre Colignon, having followed all the arguments, had sent him a note to say that he was adhering, *malgré tout, à « son » interprétation...* at which Claude, having already dismissed him as being *assez fermé aux arguments intelligents,* compounds the insult by adding, on a note of apparent despair:

> *Alors comment faire ? Les gens préfèrent le mensonge plutôt que d'avoir à réviser leur opinion.*

People are often so strongly attached to what they have been taught, and to their own certainties, that they are reluctant even to consider the possibility of being mistaken. One might argue that there is at least some logic in the belief that the origin of *croque-mort* was to be found in the supposed practice of those who wrapped the bodies of the dead in their shrouds and then bit the big toe of the corpses to verify death.   Claude disagrees:

> *Eh bien non. Ce procédé qui consiste à supposer une pratique, à imaginer une coutume, voire une anecdote, pour tenter d'expliquer l'origine d'un mot, surtout d'une expression, est beaucoup plus fréquent qu'il ne paraît.*

He concedes that there is perhaps a natural tendency to fall into such a trap, even among the most sensible and highly educated of people, and continues:

> *J'ai vu de mes yeux un académicien fameux expliquer la locution « prendre des vessies pour des lanternes » par un fait de société du XVIe siècle, alors que les prémices de cette expression sont déjà bien attestées dès le XIIIe siècle.*

Claude then brings the matter to a close, unequivocally, with a little *humour noir*:

Ajoutons que la société mondaine des années 1780 aimait à jouer bizarrement avec les mots de la mort. Au même moment se créait dans l'entourage du fringant comte d'Artois, futur Charles X, l'expression admirable : « à tombeau ouvert », pour la grande vitesse d'un carrosse. Au fond, l'invention de la guillotine, cinq ou six ans plus tard, fut peut-être l'expression suprême de cette gaieté morbide.

Another of his readers, a certain Monsieur Bazin, has raised the question of the etymology of the informal verb *bosser*, which Claude admits he would never have dreamt of researching had someone not suggested it to him. Eliminating any possible connection with the English "boss", Claude states that the verb, when used in the sense of *travailler dur*, comes from the Breton and Norman regional expression *bosser du dos*, *« faire le gros dos »*.   In the west of France, however, the meaning is *faire des bosses*, as in *« La voiture surchargée bossait de partout »*, the latter usage (found in La Varende) taken from *Robert*. That is not the end of the story, however, since, having once begun to research a word, Claude does not leave his investigation until perfectly satisfied that he has exhausted every etymological possibility. In the case of *bosser* he reports his discovery that at the end of the nineteenth century it meant something entirely different, *en antiphrase : rire, bien s'amuser* !   He is intrigued to learn how this could be so.   Again his searching bears fruit, for he finds that in the 1850s *une bosse* signified *excès de plaisir ou de débauche*, which in turn derived from an expression used in the late eighteenth century, perhaps arising from the revolutionary period when the people of Paris were starving and *se faire des bosses* or *se donner des bosses* meant having a good meal. Claude considers it possible that this expression alludes to the swollen cheeks of someone with a mouth full of food, one *qui se cale les joues*. He adds humorously: *l'aspect « hamster », si l'on veut !* In 1799, however, there was a song, Claude discovered, which implied that the rotundity may have referred more to the abdomen than to the cheeks: *« À chaque repas, j'nous f'rons des bosses au ventre »,* a ditty reminding one perhaps of the *comptine* popularised by Patrick Topaloff in 1971: « J'ai bien mangé, j'ai bien bu, j'ai la peau du ventre bien tendue—merci, petit Jésus ! ».

It is not unusual to find words evolving and eventually assuming a sense very different from their earlier meaning and sometimes directly opposed to their former sense. The verb *se marrer*, for instance, which now means to laugh uproariously, to be in stitches, once signified to be bored. Strangely enough, *se marrer* can still be found with this earlier meaning, when used ironically. A similar case is found in the French adjective *terrible*, which in familiar conversation is—and has been for many decades now—the equivalent of the English informal "fantastic, great, amazing".   Certain

English words have evolved in a similar way: *wicked,* for example, when used by the younger generation, denotes more often than not something wonderful, where there is no hint of malice.

One of Claude's faithful readers, a certain Madame Gressard of Villeurbanne, provides several examples of faulty syntax for him to consider, some of which he uses in his article *Enjambements ridicules* (2 March 1995). He opens his witty, entertaining and instructive *chronique* in this way:

> « À peine amputée de la jambe, sa voiture roula dans un ravin » *est une phrase idiote, doublée d'une catastrophe syntaxique sur fond de malchance absolue.*

With characteristic humour, Claude highlights the syntactical error of the sentence and proceeds to cite other amusing examples, among which is one taken from a newspaper report:

> *Quelquefois on assiste à du fantastique de conte de fées :* « Partie en vacances, la maison de la vieille dame fut cambriolée...» *On imagine la pauvre maison qui a pris ses congés au bord de la mer—en Bretagne, peut-être—où elle s'est juchée sur un rocher pas cher. Des voyous cupides s'introduisent dans son intérieur pour y dérober des bibelots de famille !*

After quoting and criticising the following brief example, « En quittant la terre philippine, la foule de Manille fit une ovation au Pape », Claude explains fully why this commonly found construction is so ill conceived. It is not the crowd that is leaving the Pope in Manilla but the Pope who is leaving the crowd; the Pope is not left standing there alone, clad in white robes, like Christ in the wilderness, waving goodbye to the people of Manilla as they fly off! Our *chroniqueur* continues:

> *Hélas, la féerie sera pour une autre fois : ce n'était qu'une erreur de syntaxe. La mise en apposition ne peut concerner que le sujet commun des deux propositions en présence :* « Parti *de bonne heure,* Gaspard *avait tout son temps ». Appliquer cette apposition à un autre terme dans la phrase constitue une atteinte grave à la logique du français [...] User d'un raccourci asyntaxique constitue un enjambement de pensée ridicule.*

What Claude writes here concerning the logic of French applies equally to English, where this kind of error is similarly prevalent, not only among careless speakers and writers but also among careful, educated people. Even when given an explanation of the rule, many fail to understand it and some refuse to accept it, maintaining that the sense is clear from the context—only a fool would mistake the meaning—yet to linguists and grammarians and to any who wish to promote logical thought, arguments of this nature are specious. Such a statement as "Walking along the road, the tree came into view" may well be amusing but it is nonetheless illogical and grammatically indefensible.

It has been observed by some, including George Orwell (*Politics and the English Language*, 1946), that lack of clarity in expression may well indicate an inability to reason soundly. Maurice Chapelan, Aristide, Claude's predecessor at *Le Figaro littéraire*, wrote of such syntactical failings:

> Quand il se perd une nuance de langage, il se perd une nuance d'âme ; toute défaite de la syntaxe est une défaite de l'esprit. (Chapelan, *Main courante,* 1957: 73).

Claude wonders why this type of error—*une bévue grossière*—has now become so prevalent, when such a mistake would in former times have been considered a disgrace in the writing of a twelve-year-old schoolboy. He concludes that the culprits are possibly trying to sound sophisticated and stylish, displaying

> *un curieux souci d'élégance postscolaire : le cliché qui consiste à lancer des circonstancielles en début de phrase pour donner de l'« envol » au récit.*

On 26 January 1995 Claude gave his *chronique* the title *Là gît le lièvre*. On 23 March, he returns to the same subject, this time heading his article in Latin, *Hic jacet lepus*.   We are surprised to learn that many worried readers have been writing to him, expressing their concern about something he included—so many indeed that he feels obliged to respond to their unease. Claude singles out one of his critics, a doctor from Le Havre, whom he does not name, who claims to have been astonished to witness Claude's confusion of the two verbs *gésir* and *gîter*, contrasting him unflatteringly with « les bons auteurs, dont La Fontaine, qui disent *Un lièvre en son gîte songeait* », which reference is irrelevant in the circumstances, since neither the noun *gîte* nor the verb *gîter* is the matter under review. Claude is perhaps too polite and accommodating on this occasion. The doctor exclaims: « Je me demande si l'on ne dira pas bientôt : ci-gît la langue française ».

Of course, Claude, who is not guilty of any confusion, explains that the expression is in fact an old saying: « *C'est là que gît le lièvre* »—in Latin, *hic jacet lepus*—which means « C'est là le nœud de l'affaire, le point le plus difficile ». Our *chroniqueur* asserts that the wording of old proverbs cannot be changed and continues with an explanation of the verb *gésir* (derived from the Latin *jacere*), which has all but fallen into disuse in modern French. The meaning is *être couché, être étendu par terre,* whence the wording found on epitaphs. Claude then quotes from Isaac de Benserade, the seventeenth-century court poet:

Ci-gît, oui gît, par la morbleu
Le Cardinal de Richelieu
Et ce qui cause mon ennui
Ma pension gît avec lui

and refers to the long-deceased Cardinal as the *premier de nos ministres de la Culture*. Richelieu is more often called *le premier des Premiers ministres du monde,* but Claude refers here clearly to the fact that the Cardinal was not only a leading patron of the arts but was responsible for the founding of the *Académie française*.   He goes on to provide the other meaning of *gésir*, the state of being hidden, showing how La Fontaine himself (Claude pointedly referring here to the ill-advised reproach of the doctor from Le Havre) had written:

N'ayant autre œuvre, autre emploi, penser autre
Que de chercher où gisaient les bons vins

and affirms that the saying « *Là gît le lièvre* » has its origins in hunting, commenting that the experienced huntsman conducts a cruel game with the hare, uncovering the hiding-place of the animal only then to let it free to run again until sheer exhaustion overtakes it. As for the noun *le gîte*, although it derives from the same Latin verb, it signifies the home, the place where one sleeps, thus in the context of the hare, its "form", the slight hollow the creature makes for itself in the long grass, a home providing very little protection from predators. Claude ends his *chronique* with a retort to his critics:

Certes, je suis loin d'être infaillible, et pas plus qu'un autre à l'abri d'une grosse bévue ; mais pour cette fois au moins ce sont mes censeurs [...].

Of particular etymological interest is a question he received from a reader concerning the origin of the dessert known as *les quatre mendiants*. Claude's *chronique* on this subject was reproduced in the digital edition of the newspaper on 22 December 2017:

On m'a demandé pourquoi une assiette de fruits secs servis au dessert s'appelle communément « les quatre mendiants ».

He explains that the composition of the dessert is fixed: the four *mendiants* in question are dried figs, hazelnuts, currants and almonds. Claude suggests that we may be forgiven for imagining that these four ingredients are intended for poor people, that they constitute a pudding for beggars.

> *Il n'en est rien. Ce « coquetèle » n'est d'ailleurs pas du tout négligeable, nutritivement parlant ; il se pourrait même que l'absorption d'oléagineux comme la noisette et l'amande ait pu, dans des temps anciens où l'on buvait surtout après les repas, constituer une prévention contre l'ivresse.*

Claude goes on to inform us that Plutarch and, after him, Brillat-Savarin, advised one to eat five or six bitter almonds before drinking in order to protect oneself from the effects of alcohol. He then adds a personal note, referring to some friends of his who had been in the habit of secretly drinking half a glass of cooking-oil before a heavy night out.

He returns to the matter in hand: the origin of the expression *les quatre mendiants*. First of all, it goes back to the sixteenth century, to religious orders. Explicitly, *les quatre mendiants* referred in common parlance to those orders having a vow of poverty and therefore depending entirely on alms—the Augustinians, the Carmelites, the Dominicans and the Franciscans. They are found designated in this way in *la Satyre ménippée* of 1593, in the description of a procession, where these monks occupied a position at the rear, after all the various orders. Claude quotes directly from the work:

> Après ces béats pères marchaient les quatre mendiants, qui avaient multiplié en plusieurs ordres, tant ecclésiastiques que séculiers.

In view of the significance accorded to the order of precedence in such a procession, says Claude, the fact that these four orders found themselves at the back would indicate the choice of nuts and dried fruits as food coming last on a list of dishes, though he knows that this is not the main reason for the expression. He believes that the metaphor arose from the association of the colour of the individual foods with that of the habits worn by the brothers. The Augustinians wore black, a colour akin to that of currants; the Carmelites wore dark brown, the colour of dried figs; the Franciscans wore habits of ashen hue, more or less the colour of almonds, and the Dominicans were clad in light brown, a colour resembling that of the hazelnut. Here he cannot help remarking: *Heureux temps où l'habit faisait le moine !*

He reflects on a time, two centuries earlier, when frugality did not permit people to gorge themselves on endless sweet stuff. He calls to mind Louis-Sébastien Mercier, an ardent follower of the « chymiste » Parmentier, who had invented potato bread and looked forward earnestly to an age when people would live on "chemical food". Mercier wrote in his *L'An 2440, rêve s'il en fut jamais*:

> La chymie pourra tirer un jour de tous les corps un principe nourrissant, et il sera alors aussi facile à l'homme de pourvoir à sa subsistance que de puiser l'eau dans les lacs et les fontaines.

Claude presents this as an accurate prediction of the genetically modified food products already familiar to us in the early twenty-first century. He adds, however, that today's water is in great need of « la chymie » if it is to become drinkable. He concludes his piece as follows:

> *Les quatre mendiants ? Un plat pieux, délice des végétariens, et des amateurs d'une alimentation « biologique » et naturelle !*

Another of his articles to have been prompted by a letter he has received—this time from a woman, Henriette Mathieu—is *Entre guillemets* (13 April 1995). His reader complains of the unwelcome intrusion into the spoken word of the expression « entre guillemets », which is a feature of the written word and has no place in conversation. She considers it *un tic de langage* in some people and argues that if a speaker wishes to highlight, *mettre en valeur*, a particular word or phrase there are plenty of ways of doing so vocally: *pose, ralentissement du son, intonations diverses,* without having recourse to the annoying use of « entre guillemets ». Claude does not altogether share his reader's opinion and in fact wonders whether the way people speak these days would lend itself to such vocal techniques as those she advocates... In any case, he is not at all sure that the main purpose of the expression « entre guillemets » is to underline or stress a point: he thinks not.

There is rather more to the use in speech of these typographic marks than mere highlighting. In his opinion « entre guillemets » serves to create a distance between the speaker and the word or words he or she is quoting. Claude had first noticed this use among Americans and had subsequently witnessed it in England in the 1960s, when he had observed people in London, especially those of an artistic inclination, raising their hands to their heads and using their fingers to form quotation marks in the air, simultaneously saying "quote", as if to confirm the authenticity of what they were saying and to declare that they were reporting the actual words they had heard, *ipsissima verba*, and not their own opinion.

In his summary Claude suggests that « entre guillemets » may mark a degree of caution and reserve, in that those using it may intend to disassociate themselves from what they are citing, showing a reluctance to be identified with the original speaker:

> *La formulation évite l'aspect catégorique d'un jugement, elle introduit le doute, permettant de dire sans dire, tout en disant… Or, la modernité ne tend-elle pas à favoriser le flou, l'ambigu ?—Au fond, c'est là une locution, entre guillemets,* perverse, *qui est bien adaptée au temps !*

Thus Claude has taken up and turned to his own advantage a reader's opinion, which has inspired him to analyse humorously, with more than a tinge of gentle sarcasm, what has now become a common usage. One may well imagine Madame Mathieu's disappointment on reading the *chronique*.

In his *En avant la musique* (8 May 1997) he refers to a letter received from one of his readers who also happens to listen to *France-Musique*: this man has been *ahuri par le scandale*, utterly shocked by a usage with which Claude himself had not previously been acquainted:

> *[…] c'est que sur cette prestigieuse chaîne de radio, haut-lieu du goût musical, on dit maintenant, comme en anglais : Untel joue* le *violon, joue* la *trompette, et non plus comme en français : « Il joue* du *violon, du* piano, *de la* cornemuse *»… Je dois reconnaître que la nouvelle me coupe le sifflet !*

He chooses here the expression *la nouvelle me coupe le sifflet*, with its double meaning, though, having already reported in that same *chronique* that sports commentators no longer speak of football teams playing *contre* one another, preferring to use the English construction, *ils jouent Bordeaux,* Claude should perhaps not have been unduly surprised to encounter a similar change of construction with reference to the playing of musical instruments. He may well love the English language but he objects to its all-pervading presence in the media and bemoans its damaging influence on the French language:

> *La puissance médiatique est là, énorme rouleau compresseur de notre syntaxe, nous n'y échapperons pas.*

He admits that there is no escaping the inevitable and amuses us with his apt choice of metaphor, likening the ineluctable, inexorable, crushing effect of the media—in other words, of the English language (or more usually the American)—on French syntax to that of a gigantic steam-roller, an unstoppable force.

In *Plaidoyer pour un banni* (2005: 179) Claude refers to the expression *Je m'excuse*, which is widely used, though sometimes censured by grammarians and often the butt of jokes: anyone saying *Je m'excuse* should expect the *repartie, qui se veut cinglante* : « Laissez-moi ce soin ! » One of his readers, J-P Martin, recounts his own recent experience, his *mésaventure*, as he jocularly calls it. During a meeting with friends (« du moins je les croyais tels ») he had unwisely offered a defence of the expression *Je m'excuse*, and, as a result of his imprudent attempt, he was so ill treated by his friends that he exclaims in amazement: « Que n'avais-je pas dit là ? Je sens bien que je suis maintenant au ban de la société ».

Although Claude himself has no objection to the expression, he feels obliged by his reader's letter to ask himself the question: *où est le problème* ? Maurice Grevisse and his son-in-law, André Goosse, who has compiled *Le Bon Usage* since the death of Grevisse, provide an explanation of *Je m'excuse* which satisfies Claude. The common criticism of the expression is founded on a mistaken belief that it is a shortened form of *Je me pardonne à moi-même*. Claude realises that such an explanation is entirely false, since *Je m'excuse* is so obviously a conflation of several statements: « Je vous présente mes excuses, je vous prie de m'excuser, car voici mes raisons », for example. It is simply a useful formula, a convenient abbreviation.

There is another meaning, devoid of any sense of apology or regret, to be seen in the *Je m'excuse « de contradiction »*, introducing an argument or expressing a difference of opinion:

> « Vous dites que vous étiez cinq cents ? Je m'excuse, je vous ai comptés : il n'y avait que trois cents participants, mon cher Rodrigue ! »...*Bien sûr, c'est là du langage parlé ; mais quoi ? Il existe aussi celui-là et, pour être du registre familier, il n'en est pas moins de bon aloi. Du moins, c'est mon opinion.*

This last comment is typical of Claude's views on the French language. Popular usage, *le registre familier*, is of supreme importance to him and is a recurring theme in his writing. In the *chronique* we considered earlier, *Là gît le lièvre*, he treats the subject in detail, expressing his regret that French, unlike other European languages, did not develop naturally from the language of the people but was created artificially by and for an élite. The fact is, Claude maintains, that its evolution was dictated by socio-political conditions in the seventeenth century, when the French language became detached from the common tongue:

> *Elle a, dès cette époque, évolué à grande vitesse à l'intérieur d'un cercle élitaire axé sur la Cour et sa banlieue d'influence* […]

On another occasion, he has received from an elderly reader, a certain Monsieur Andreu of Toulouse, a query regarding the use of *en vélo*, which the reader had noticed, much to his surprise, on the front page of *Le Figaro*. He had been taught at school that the only correct expression is *à vélo*. The question is of interest to Claude, more for his correspondent's background than for the linguistic point he raises, of which he seems eventually to have lost track. The letter prompts his *chronique* (21 October 1994), *À pied, à cheval, et en vélo*. Monsieur Andreu had written :

> J'ai quatre-vingts ans, j'ai appris le français à la communale d'un village catalan où mes parents parlaient le catalan, mais où notre langue était interdite sous peine de sanctions.

This situation, only too familiar to Claude himself, as we have seen, had in fact been the experience of the majority of French people born between the two wars, when the process of imposing the French language as the norm throughout the land was nearing its completion. Monsieur Andreu asks:

> Alors, doit-on dire *à vélo* ou *en vélo* ? Mon redoutable instituteur tenait à ce qu'on emploie *à vélo* sous peine de recevoir un coup de pied au cul dont il avait le secret.

The status of regional languages was a matter of particular concern to Claude, as we learn from his *Parler croquant* (1973), and the situation described by his reader explains the present weak position of the French language internationally, according to our *chroniqueur*: the transplant had not taken root sufficiently well. *Mais revenons à nos pédales.*

Claude explains the history of the use of *en* with vehicles of all kinds:

> *Le* en *n'est pas un descriptif intérieur-extérieur, il joue un rôle purement instrumental : on dira* en *pour tout nouveau moyen de locomotion,* en *tricycle si la machine a trois roues,* en *side-car, et aussi, par pure logique fonctionnelle,* en *tandem (et jamais à tandem). Cela montre bien que dans l'esprit du locuteur* en *n'a pas la connotation* dedans-dehors *mais seulement « par le moyen de »...*

He goes on to stress the same point, illustrating with his customary humour that the use of *en* does not depend on the type of vehicle in question but is correctly found with any kind of vehicle:

> *On dit* en *traîneau,* en *tapis volant, s'il le faut—des véhicules dépourvus d'intérieur. Se rendre quelque part* en *vélo n'est donc pas une hérésie grammaticale comme le pensait le maître d'école de Monsieur Andreu ; c'est*

seulement une manière agréable, pratique et pas chère de se déplacer, en ville comme à la campagne. À vélo, sur le modèle de à bicyclette est hérité de à cheval sans nécessité, par une sorte de complaisance au code dominant.

What Claude says here concerning the legitimate place of the spoken word again typifies his stance. He considers that the present insistence on the use of *à vélo* has come about through hypercorrection among *les gens avisés*, influenced in childhood by their schoolmasters: this phenomenon has ousted the form *en vélo,* which he insists is linguistically quite correct. The same applies to *en moto.* Claude closes his *chronique* with a word of advice to his reader, though he seems to have forgotten that the original query had in fact concerned the use of *en vélo,* rather than the expression *à vélo,* which his elderly correspondent had been so firmly and strictly taught at school:

> *Si je puis résumer mon sentiment, je conseillerai à Monsieur Andreu de continuer à dire en vélo puisqu'il s'agit du moyen de transport, et à vélo dans les cas où il est fait spécifiquement allusion à la notion d'équilibre, comme :* « Cet enfant sait déjà se tenir *à vélo.* » *Du moins, c'est mon sentiment.*

We have seen before such closing comments. Claude is never didactic; on the contrary, he is anxious to point out, modestly, that what he writes is only his opinion: *Du moins, c'est mon opinion* and, as here, *Du moins, c'est mon sentiment.*

Many of Claude's *chroniques* were prompted by readers' questions, and to some of these we shall inevitably return. The next chapter, however, will deal with a matter of particular linguistic interest to him: everyday language.

CHAPTER TWO

LE LANGAGE DE TOUS LES JOURS

> *C'est ce nom qui est drôle,* Navigo, *autour duquel il est fait une grande publicité.*
> —Claude Duneton, *Le Navigo au pays des Parigots, c'est de l'argot !* reproduced in *Le Figaro—Langue française* on 13 July 2017.

The sounds of language, its forms, its origins and its quirks all feature in Claude Duneton's writings, As we know, it is above all words, *les mots,* including those of *l'argot, le langage populaire* and *le langage familier,* that are his enduring passion.

He wittily gives his article the title *Le Navigo au pays des Parigots, c'est de l'argot !* and introduces it thus:

> *L'administration se déboutonne ; c'est du moins l'impression que donnent les Transports parisiens, qui ont créé le* Navigo *comme mode de paiement— une carte à puce qui fait « bip » lorsque l'usager des métro, RER, bus la présente à l'appareil décodeur, ce qui s'appelle « valider ».*

He reminds his readers that the sound [o] at the end of a word is ambiguous in French, as it appears in more than one register.   The spelling may be *o* or *ot* but the sound is the same: it is found in prestigious Italian or Latin words such as *primo, allegro, impresario* as well as in familiar slang, in the form of abbreviations: *cuistot, poivrot* (formerly used of *poivre*)*,* and in the indispensable *apéro.* He tells us:

> *Du temps où il y avait des ouvriers métallurgistes, ils se désignaient eux-mêmes affectueusement comme des* métallos—*il existe à Paris une* Maison des métallos, *devenue un théâtre. Les musiciens de jazz ou de variété se désignent comme des* musicos, *et les Parisiens s'appellent toujours des* Parigots.

Claude provides examples of fashionable abbreviations such as *intello, la déco, un dico, un macho* and tells us that *un parano* is someone always fearing the worst for himself, short for the medical term « paranoïaque », whereas *le mégalo* is an individual for whom nothing is important unless it relates to him, short for « mégalomane ». In good *chroniqueur* fashion he now further exemplifies, humorously, what he has stated:

> *En gros—je dirai même* grosso modo—*le* o *final fait peuple, ou comme disait le philosophe Gabriel Marcel pour stigmatiser une connotation populacière, le* o *« sent l'ail »* !

The case of *le collabo* is rather different.   This word existed before the Second World War, of course, but since then it has acquired a strongly pejorative meaning, rather as *le facho* in politics is the undesirable reminder of fascism.   There are also *les socialos*, those legendary members of the working classes who fought for the great causes of the past.   If there is one term, however, which has had a particularly noxious career, it is *le collabo*. The word goes back to the 1920s, when it signified in familiar language any fellow-worker in any situation:

> *« Je vous présente un jeune collabo » se disait aussi simplement, avant 1940, que de nos jours « voici le nouvel assistant de Dominique ». Mais plus en 1945 ! Diable non ! Le collaborateur ayant été celui qui avait opté inconsidérément pour la « collaboration » avec l'Allemagne des nazis, on continua à parler de* collabo, *mais dans   un   sens odieusement chargé de « traître », et dans le monde « résistant », d'immonde salopard !*

In what follows one may detect Claude's personal feelings: the former colleague was now, in 1945, either spat upon in the office, or shot at Vincennes, depending on the degree of influence he had enjoyed during the Occupation.   That explains why, when the full word « collaborateur » resumed its usual meaning, its abbreviation remained unacceptable.

What, though, of *Navigo*?   Why had the RATP chosen this strange word? What could lie behind such a choice?   Claude assumes the word is an abbreviation of *navigateur,* or the English equivalent, the name implying that the card in question allows passengers to travel on any form of public transport available in the Paris region:

> *Ma parole d'honneur, c'est une formation argotique ! Mais si, une création parfaitement désinvolte : Navigo, comme démago ! C'est rigolo... Presque écolo, à l'oreille. Qui donc a proposé ce mot à la RATP ? Une agence de com' ? J'aurais voulu être une petite souris pour assister aux débats qui ont entériné le terme.*

In mocking tone Claude expresses his surprise that the RATP should have accepted such a term, as it is most definitely slang.   He imagines the use of

Navigo, pronounced with an *accent faubourien* in an expression such as « *Dis donc, on m'a barboté mon Navigo !* » which might be found in one of Jacques Audiard's films. His several musings on the word even include the possibility of a sexual connotation, whereupon he promptly stops his reflections and declares: *Oui, Navigo, mon pote, c'est de l'argot !*

Returning to the [o] sound—this time with the spelling *ot*—in his article *Boulot ? Mais quel boulot ?* (14 September 2000), Claude says that the word *boulot*, although of relatively recent date—no earlier than 1880—seems to have become the everyday equivalent of *travail* and is used with that meaning by people of all ages and all levels of education. Before 1900 it was spelt as the birch tree, *bouleau,* and was first recorded in 1894 in the *Dictionnaire de l'argot fin de siècle* by Charles Virmaître, who gave it as a neologism. Virmaître stated that the word originated from the language of wood-carvers, who needed birch for their work, a derivation completely at odds with that later attributed to it by linguists. Claude quotes Virmaître:

> Cette expression s'est étendue à tous les corps de métier qui disent : « Je cherche du bouleau (Argot du peuple) ».

He finds it unlikely that such a narrow, minority use should have spread to all manner of work, especially when it is attested nowhere other than in Virmaître. Claude wonders whether there has been some confusion with the word *boulot* as found slightly later in the work of the writer Hector France:

> « On appelle *boulot* dans l'argot des ateliers l'œuvre d'art, marbre, plâtre ou tableau qui reste pour compte au comité chargé d'organiser le salon. Et *le cimetière des boulots* n'est autre que le vaste garde-meuble situé avenue de Saxe, où depuis de longues années viennent s'entasser les œuvres qui n'ont point été réclamées après que le Salon a fermé ses portes » (Dictionnaire de la langue verte, *publié vers 1907, qui cite ce terme seulement dans son Appendice et ignore les autres sens ou orthographes).*

Having made little progress in his search for the true origin of the word, Claude asks: *Alors d'où sort notre « petit boulot » ?*

The spread of the word from the very restricted setting of wood-carving seems all the more implausible to him when he discovers a song, dating from 1892, which contains the word *boulot* in the context of work in general: « au lieu d'gouaper (voler) je m'f'rais boulot ». This quotation he found in the work of Gaston Esnault, the Breton linguist and *argot* specialist.

He tells us that modern commentators follow Esnault in interpreting *boulot* as a « déverbal de boulotter » on the basis of *Ça boulotte,* meaning *ça tourne, ça roule, ça va bien*, an expression supplanted around 1915 by *ça gaze*, following the progress of the external combustion engine. The verb *boulotter* is a simple diminutive of *bouler*, known from 1800 and defined by the lexicographer, Lorédan Larchey, in 1862 as « vivre dans une sorte d'aisance » and by Alfred Delvau in 1867, similarly, as « aller doucement, faire de petites affaires ».   The verb was used equally in the sense of succeeding: « fructifier, prospérer, faire la boule de neige », and we find in Balzac: « Il resterait donc cent mille francs à faire boulotter ».

There is, however, Claude informs us, another meaning of *boulotter*, as old as the one just mentioned but quite distinct from it: « manger », dating from the 1840s and still found in current slang. There is a semantic overlap here with another—forgotten—*boulot* : *le pain boulot*, in other words *la boule de pain*. This usage was known from *le second Empire*. If Robert did not include it until 1896, Claude assures us of its prior existence:

> *J'ai là, sous mes yeux, un texte de 1872 qui en fait foi. Je le livre en prime aux lexicographes :* Les Femmes de France pendant la guerre *(de 1870 !) par Paul et Henry de Trailles, Paris, F. Polo libraire-éditeur 1872. La citation est la suivante :* « Le ménage vivait à l'aise avant la guerre. On avait le charbon, le bois et le vin à la cave, le linge en piles dans l'armoire, l'argenterie au panier. Chaque matin, le boulanger envoyait le pain boulot, jocko (pain long) ou en couronne ».

We surely agree with Claude that there is in such an etymology a happy coincidence of the bread we eat and the work we do in order to buy it. He ends wittily:

> « *Chercher du boulot* », *serait-ce* « *chercher un boulot* » *?...Hasard ou étymologie possible ? Ah, quel travail !*

Remaining in the realm of food, we come to *la bouffe*, which is often associated with over-indulgence. Claude reminds us in his article *Et la bouffe vint...* (19 June 1997) of the old proverb which warns us that *les excès* make us « creuser la tombe avec les dents ». The success of the noun *la bouffe*, which is of dialectal origin, and not slang, grew during the twentieth century and, as Claude tells us:

> [...] *explosa littéralement en 1973 avec la vogue du film de Marco Ferreri,* La Grande Bouffe.

The cinema firmly established *la bouffe* among people of all ages and classes, but the word has an exemplary history.   It is usually considered a recent item of vocabulary but, Claude claims, *il est vieux comme la pluie*.

The more reliable dictionaries of unconventional terms give 1925 as the date of emergence of the expression *la bouffe*, indicating that this vulgar-sounding word had spread through the population when the soldiers had returned home from the war, since between 1914 and 1918 there had been an enormous mix of language and culture among *les poilus*. Claude finds this explanation unlikely, as those who, like René Benjamin, Henri Barbusse and Gaston Esnault, had made a record of language used on the battle-field, had failed to note *la bouffe*. The word had appeared, however, as early as 1914 in a song written by Théodore Botrel, sung to a popular tune, which, according to my research, may have been that used for the comptine *La voilà, la jolie vigne*:

Que tous en bouffent,
La voilà la jolie bouffe,
Bouffi, bouffo, bouffons le Boche
La voilà la jolie bouffe aux Boches,
La voilà la jolie bouffe !

Claude, yet more delighted to have found an even earlier instance of the word, writes:

Mais la surprise que j'ai eue, au cours de mes longues veilles studieuses, fut de rencontrer la bouffe *cent ans auparavant, à la date faramineuse de 1823 ! À cette date, Madame de Genlis, dont on sait combien elle fut une observatrice attentive des façons de parler de son temps, écrivait dans* Les Veillées de la chaumière *(un titre parodié par la suite), ce dialogue dialectal entre un paysan champenois et le comte local :*
JÉRÔME : Je ne suis pas ivrogne de mon naturel, et je n'aime ni la boisson ni la bouffe.
TIBURCE : Tu as bien raison, car la bouffe et la boisson donnent de terribles maladies... Mais ne différons plus, allons finir notre vendange.

That brief dialogue shows how certain words can circulate for centuries in the spoken language, in rural communities; absent from literature, and leave few traces of themselves for the historical linguist, for whom precise dating remains a perennial problem.

Leaving aside *la bouffe*, Claude bemoans the fact that

[...] nous avons disposé par le passé, depuis toujours, de gigantesques réservoirs idiomatiques, constitués par la masse des dialectes parlés dans la nation : la flotte, *apparue vers les années 1890, est un autre exemple. Qu'en sera-t-il dorénavant ?*

Now that regional languages have all but disappeared and much popular language has atrophied, along with a traditional way of life, what reserves do we have at our disposal? Claude wonders how it will be in the twenty-first century: where will people find the essence, *le sel*, of idiomatic expression, imagery and colourful turns of phrase? Will the French language find itself at the mercy of those strict *commissions de terminologie*? Will it never enjoy the freedom to blossom in its natural habitat? The future looks bleak, though it must be said that *la flotte* is still very much in evidence.

An extraordinary compound noun, a familiar term and one that never fails to shock serious students of French, is the ubiquitous « auto-école », a construction alien to the *génie de la langue*. When analysed it does not mean what it is intended to convey: driving-school, school of motoring. How did this strangely formed word come into the language? My own opinion is that it was probably a crude *calque* of "motor school", which was the term in current use in England during the early decades of the twentieth century. Why do the French prefer it to the more natural term « école de conduite »?

Claude considers the matter in his long article *Auto-école* (30 October 1997), reproduced in the digital edition of *Le Figaro* on 4 November 2016:

> *Songe-t-on parfois à l'imbroglio sémantico-syntaxique de cette construction à laquelle nous sommes accoutumés au point de ne plus la voir ? À force de pratiquer les formules du genre* auto-allumage, auto-discipline, auto-surveillance, *nous considérons le préfixe* « auto » *comme signifiant seulement* « par soi-même ».

As he ponders the question, Claude wonders whether, on seeing « auto-école » marked on the slowly moving car in front of us, we imagine that people are teaching themselves. Of course not! We all understand perfectly well that « auto-école » is a school for people learning to drive. Everyone who reads the word knows that learner-drivers are being taught motoring skills and how to behave on the road. Claude then teases his readers further:

> *Pourquoi ? Parce que le substantif* auto, *qui fut l'apocope ordinaire d'usage commun de 1910 à 1950 d'*automobile, *est devenu, dans la réalité d'aujourd'hui, pratiquement obsolète. Rares sont les gens en France à part la génération des conducteurs âgés de soixante-quinze à quatre-vingt-dix ans, et leurs épouses qui disent spontanément :* « Nous allons faire une promenade en auto », *ou bien :* « L'auto a refusé de se mettre en route ».

In modern France the word *auto* conjures up the image of an "old banger" with lots of chrome, a running-board and a boxy, upright body, reminiscent of those parked outside a veteran car club. These days the French use the word *voiture* or a familiar term such as *bagnole*, in accordance with their age and linguistic preference. Nevertheless, although the word *automobile* and its abbreviated form have fallen into disuse, they have remained in the collective consciousness of the people. Claude considers that the word *auto* covers the semantic field rather as a lace table cloth covers a *guéridon*. The word embraces the *espace automobile*, and that means that the *auto* of *auto-école* loses its normal function of the Greek prefix, *tout seul*, to embody the school in the mechanical field of driving. That is all well and good, says Claude, but this is an example of English syntax. It is the wrong way round; in French it should be *école-auto*, but that now shocks the ear. He then attempts to justify *auto-école*, though without great conviction:

> *Qu'en est-il en réalité de notre* auto-école *? Eh bien oui, c'est bel et bien* une auto *dans l'acception surannée dont je viens d'indiquer l'effacement. Ce véhicule n'est pas une « école » où l'on enseigne la conduite, mais une auto qui sert d'école. Ouf ! la syntaxe est sauve ! [...] La preuve en est que son homologue aquatique s'appelle un* bateau-école *(et non une* école bateau *!). Certes !... un substantif à temps plein.*

What should be said, however, of the little shop next door to the driving-school office, where the *Code de la route* is taught? That teaching-space also advertises in its window *auto-école*. Claude continues:

> *Ah donc ! nous revoici dans les délicatesses. Celle-là n'est pas une «* auto *», mais une «* école *». Et nous retombons dans le cas de figure de la syntaxe anglo-saxonne, avec* les cuir-center [*sic*] *et autres monstruosités.*

He concludes that the compound noun *auto-école* is the result of *un glissement de sens* and has become an accepted word in its entirety, the two elements becoming inseparable, a fact which makes the hyphen not only welcome but essential. Claude closes his *chronique* humorously:

> *Ce que nous venons de faire, cher lecteur, c'est tout simplement une promenade étymologique en auto ! On parle d'« archéologie industrielle », eh bien, appelons cela un exercice d'étymologie industrielle. Déjà !*

It should please all lovers of the French language to know that *école de conduite* seems to have gained some ground in recent years.

In his article *L'anglais ou les ingrédients d'un bon slogan,* dated 14 October 2007 and republished on 14 April 2017 by *Le Figaro* in its electronic newspaper, Claude quotes another example of syntax which is completely alien to the French language. In an advertisement displayed on every wall in Paris a bank announced: « No paperasses génération ».   The slogan appeared under the photograph of a pleasant-looking young man, informally but smartly dressed and sporting an open-neck shirt, who was throwing papers up in the air, clearly proclaiming the "paperless generation", the society we were all promised a few decades ago, coinciding with the advent of computer technology, word-processing and electronic mail. Although *paperasses* is undoubtedly French and the accents are preserved in the word *génération*, the slogan is not French, being incapable of grammatical analysis. The company in question, the Internet bank *monabanq* [*sic*], uses two French words in a three-word slogan but has chosen to couch its publicity message in a foreign construction. On the other hand, the bid submitted by Paris for the 2024 Olympic Games, "Made for sharing", used an English phrase containing absolutely no French at all. What this says about the future of the French language is a matter of speculation... One must concede, however, that the slogan worked well, as Paris was chosen to host *les Jeux olympiques 2024.*

Leaving aside the influence of English syntax, we turn to Claude's article *Histoire de rigoler* (9 November 2000), in which he supplies the status and history of the verb, which is not only one of the oldest recorded in the French language but is still as hale and hearty as ever. We first find its noun, *le rigolage*, around 1275, in the *Roman de la rose* by Jean de Meung, where it has the sense of « réjouissance » applied particularly to the pleasure of dancing, though it is difficult, says Claude, to separate the fun and frolics of dancing from laughter itself, which, as he reminds us, is the distinguishing feature of human beings. Moving on to the verb, he writes:

> *Disons que « rigoler », à l'ancienne, tel qu'il apparaît dans Maître Pathelin ou dans Rabelais, décrit des amusements qui incluent obligatoirement les éclats de rire.*

Not only in the fifteenth century is the verb attested; we find it in the sixteenth, too, in its reflexive form, *se rigoler*, in Nicot, where the expression *se rigoler d'aucun* (i.e., *se rigoler de quelqu'un*) is a synonym of *se gaudir*, meaning « se moquer par jeu et en riant ». As Claude points out: *On ne saurait être plus clair : rire d'autrui.*

It is noteworthy that this example did not suffer the fate of other popular words; for some obscure reason it escaped the stifling effect of the seventeenth-century *monde précieux*, possibly because the *juristes* of the French language were, like Vaugelas, too often completely unaware of *le francien*, which was the ordinary language in active use in the Île de France, where they had installed their court. The verb continued to be used, especially in its reflexive form, in the world of everyday speech. Furetière quoted it at the end of that century (1690):

> Rigoler, verbe neutre qui ne se dit qu'avec le pronom personnel. Faire une petite desbauche, manger et se réjouir entre amis. Ce terme est populaire.

The Jesuit *Dictionnaire de Trévoux* of 1771, which still had the noun *rigolage*, « vieux terme », no longer listed the verb *rigoler*. On the other hand, we find it again, in all its fullness, in the *Dictionnaire comique* of Philibert Le Roux of 1750:

> se rigoler, pour se divertir, danser, sauter, faire de petites folies réjouissantes, se gauberger [*sic*] sur l'herbe, badiner, niaiser, folâtrer.

It is quite remarkable that the word has retained its original character throughout its long history. It is repeated intact in nineteenth-century slang dictionaries such as the *Dictionnaire de la langue verte* of Alfred Delvau (1867): « s'amuser, se réjouir, boire, danser, rire, dans l'argot du peuple ».

La rigolade, a popular "re-suffixation" of the old form *le rigolage*, seems to date from the late eighteenth century. Esnault had found the word in *La chanson du malfaiteur Winter,* dated 1815, where it has all the nuances of the traditional meaning. The term would flourish in the twentieth century with « les parties de rigolade » which exemplify and highlight the authentic sense of hilarity.

Around 1840 the adjective *rigolo* appeared in popular Parisian usage, originating in workshops, where the fashionable suffix *ot* was all the rage. It is strange to note that *rigolo* served as both masculine and feminine in its early days. The word appeared in 1869 in *Le Petit Citateur*, a very unusual dictionary by the songwriter Jules Choux:

> Ce mot qui vient de rigoler dans le langage populaire, est de deux genres et du plus mauvais. Il s'applique aux personnes et aux choses : Arnal est un acteur rigolo et Thérésa une chanteuse rigolo.

At the very end of the nineteenth century the noun *le rigolo* is found in Virmaître (1894) with its meaning in criminals' slang of a burglar's jemmy:

> Elle est rigolo pour le voleur car avec l'argent volé il peut se payer de la rigolade.

Claude refers to the feminine form of the adjective, *rigolote*, which was still rare before the First World War, and to the popular expression « rigoler comme une baleine », which was already current before 1914 and found in the writings of Alphonse Allais at the turn of the century. We witness the delight of our *chroniqueur* as he discovers in his research traces of the popular speech of the past still encountered in the twenty-first century.

From time to time he discusses a purely grammatical point: the one in question here relates to the mistaken use of the subjunctive with *après que*, as a result of confusion with its correct use after *avant que*. He deals with this matter in a *chronique* dated 27 November 2008, under the heading *Y a-t-il un « avant » et un « après » ?*

Having introduced his article with a brief exposé of the major difference in character between the indicative and subjunctive moods, he remarks:

> *Il ne faut pas dire du mal du subjonctif, il faut l'aimer ; c'est un garde-fou plus subtil qu'on ne l'imagine.*

He then moves on to a particular case of difficulty, « celui qui résulte de l'antériorité d'une situation par rapport à une autre », and illustrates it thus:

> « *D'ici à ce que nous arrivions (subjonctif), il fera nuit.» L'arrivée elle-même est encore indéterminée, l'action flotte et appelle le subjonctif ; « d'ici à ce que nous arriverons » est barbare et choque très justement l'oreille. Formulé autrement : « Il fera nuit avant que nous arrivions.»*

In effect, until the action is completed the outcome is uncertain. « Il gardait de l'espoir avant qu'il soit condamné » implies that he would not necessarily be condemned. Claude then adds an important comment:

> *Notez que la correspondance des temps voudrait que l'on dise : avant qu'il fût condamné, mais l'usage familier tolère cet accroc aux bons principes.*

Thus *l'usage familier, le langage de tous les jours,* is more important in the end than grammatical accuracy; anyone using the imperfect subjunctive in speech in order to obey the rules of tense sequence—*la concordance des temps*—would sound strangely pedantic.

Explaining how in modern French the verb following *avant que* is always in the subjunctive, and is often accompanied by *ne,* as in « Fichons le camp avant qu'il (ne) pleuve », Claude wittily warns us that the problem arises after the rain!... He asks whether we must—or whether we can—say « nous repartirons après que l'orage soit passé »: that is the question. Normally, when an event has taken place, it is no longer hypothetical or imaginary, and logic dictates that, when one thing happens after another, there is no longer any doubt about it and the subjunctive has no place in the construction. He adds, however, that despite all the condemnations of grammarians people still use the subjunctive in such sentences as « L'enfant pleurait après qu'il soit tombé dans les orties »—or, when writing, « après qu'il fût tombé », with a circumflex for good measure. This would of course be an example of the correct use of a past anterior, were it not for the accent!

Claude then quotes the opinion of André Goosse, who has for many years revised and edited the famous grammar, *Le Bon Usage*, written originally by his father-in-law Maurice Grevisse:

> On observe une tendance, surtout forte depuis le deuxième tiers du XXe siècle, à faire suivre « après que » du subjonctif.

Goosse cites Sartre: « Autrefois, longtemps *après qu'elle m'ait quitté* » (on s'attendrait à *qu'elle m'eut quitté—sans l'accent*). He gives further examples from Montherlant, Duhamel, Mauriac and Camus, and quotes many other fine writers and speakers, including François Mitterrand, who said on the radio « après qu'il ait reçu certains accords ». As Claude remarks: « Voilà qui est consolant pour les étourdis ! » and for everyone else, we may add.

Duneton states his opinion that the use of the subjunctive following *après que* is the result of hypercorrection: after all, the subjunctive lends such an air of beauty, elegance and precision to the language, that one's guard is lowered and one considers the subjunctive more distinguished than a simple indicative: « Sa mère le lave après qu'il soit rentré », is far more stylish than « après qu'il est rentré ». People feel that the construction is parallel to the other, « avant que ». He states: « Une locution glisse sur l'autre, il se produit ce que j'appellerai un *courant d'air grammatical* » and closes his *chronique* with the quip: *Mais bien sûr, il faut se préserver autant qu'on le peut des courants d'air !*

It would not be fitting to leave *le langage de tous les jours* without reference to the question of when to address one's interlocutor as *tu* and when to use *vous*. Despite all the advice found in manuals of etiquette and the rules expounded in grammars, it is often a most challenging area, not only for foreigners but often for the French themselves. Duneton treats the matter in his *Quand tutoyer ou vouvoyer ?* reproduced on 5 May 2017:

> *En réalité, l'usage du* tu *et du* vous *a toujours été un sujet délicat chez les Français, voire une cause d'embarras. Selon les lieux et les époques, on ne sait jamais si c'est le vouvoiement ou le tutoiement qui crée le problème. L'incertitude est tellement essentielle qu'on n'est même pas sûr s'il s'agit de* vouvoiement *ou de* voussoiement, *ce qui est rarissime en français. Le premier est de très loin le plus courant, tandis que* voussoiement, *le préféré de Littré, paraît plus habillé.*

According to our *chroniqueur*, who has set the confused scene, summarising the problem quite succinctly, there have never been any strict rules, only special instances of usage, which have not been stable and have sometimes required fine judgment, except during *les folies révolutionnaires*, where the use of *tu* was obligatory for all, *sous peine de prison*.

Duneton states that the ambiguity of choice between the familiar *tu*, which represents the opposite of the respectful distance created by the use of *vous*, is one of the delights of the language, one of its true charms. It is simplistic to expect to be able to systematise the usage, as the choices made, instinctively or by calculation or by tradition, are subject to far too many exceptions and are capable of too many transgressions. In letter-writing people sometimes go to extreme lengths to avoid having to make the choice.

He remarks that the use of *tu* is often indicative of a group-identity and shows a certain *esprit de corps*. In the army, in journalism, among hospital staff, among actors and artists, the familiar *tu* is normal. On the other hand, some groups ban the familiar use: it was the rule in the nineteenth century that the *compagnons du Tour de France* should address one another as *vous*. Claude says: *Le* vous *serait finalement l'adresse la plus individualiste...*

These days customs can be even more difficult to understand: if it is the case that friends say *tu* to one another, especially friends of the same sex, it is equally true that many people, who can be very close friends and just as affectionate, use *vous*, especially where there is a substantial difference in age. Although families where children say *vous* to their parents have become rare, they still exist, following a middle-class tradition which was quite well known in country areas not long ago. In former days many peasants used *vous* as their normal form of address and it was not unusual, a few decades ago, for a woman to address her husband formally, whereas he called her *tu*. Duneton suggests that couples who say *vous* to each other have an advantage over those using *tu*:

> [...] *au moment des effusions intimes le soudain passage au* tu *amplifie délicieusement l'érotisme. (Cela étant, on ne dispose pas de données précises, car peu de linguistes se glissent en tiers dans un lit conjugal.)*

He appreciates the variety available in French: the difference between *le* tu *de majesté* in « Ô seigneur, toi qui règnes dans les cieux ! » and *le tu un peu crapule* as in « Toi, petit saligaud, tu me le paieras ». There is no single rationale. The combinations are endless, depending on the time and the inclination of each person. It is a sphere of freedom, where the choices available are individual, generous and meaningful: *protégeons-les !*

CHAPTER THREE

LE PASSÉ SIMPLE AND *L'IMPARFAIT DU SUBJONCTIF*

Le passé simple est devenu, pour ainsi dire, un passé « surpassé », coupé du réel. Que faire pour le ranimer ? Il n'existe à ma connaissance qu'une seule thérapie : l'employer, l'employer encore, l'employer à toutes les personnes aussi souvent que l'on peut, puisque par une incroyable ténacité de vieil animal... il respire encore !
—Claude Duneton, *Il respire encore,* 13 March 1997, *Le Figaro littéraire*

In his *Un passé trop simple* (6 March 1997) Claude Duneton provides a history of the two main past tenses in French: *le passé simple* and *le passé composé*. He explains the evolution of the two, pointing out that *simple* here does not indicate lack of difficulty but rather that the tense consists of a single part, as opposed to the two parts making up the *passé composé*, the compound tense, made up of an auxiliary verb and a past participle.

The single-word past tense, *je lus, je courus*, indicates a precise action, a completed action, precisely located in the past: « Je courus vers l'autobus qui démarrait ». Oddly, this one-word, convenient, useful tense, the past historic, once used so frequently, has now completely disappeared from the everyday spoken language. The gradual process of its demise began around the end of the eighteenth century, since when the tense has been finally relegated to the written language. No one says in conversation: « Hier, il s'éveilla à cinq heures » or « Je pris le train de 19 h 57 ».

The *passé composé*, the perfect tense, has, theoretically, a relatively limited role in syntax. « Normalement », says Claude, it is used for actions which have taken place within a stated period of time: « Il nous a rendu visite trois fois le mois dernier » or to denote an event whose effect has continued into the present time: « Il est arrivé hier »—and he is still with us. He adds:

À cette nuance se rattache les usages du type : « Jésus est né à Bethléem »—cette naissance fameuse fait de la petite ville de Judée un lieu remarquable dont le rayonnement n'a pas encore tout à fait cessé.

The perfect has now effectively taken the place of the simple past tense, not only in speech but also quite often in writing.   Claude considers it strange that French should be the only European language to have lost its simple past tense, the preterite, and finds it difficult to determine the reasons for this surprising fact.

It has been suggested that the heaviness of the preterite, particularly in the *nous* and *vous* forms, has brought about its demise, but Claude does not agree. Instead, he shares the opinion of Grevisse, who states:

> C'est prendre la conséquence pour la cause : ces formes n'étaient pas moins complexes quand elles étaient bien vivantes.

Claude goes so far as to say that the simple past is very often both lighter and more elegant than the perfect:

> « Nous partîmes cinq cents » (ou « à huit heures »), *est beaucoup plus élégant à l'oreille que* « Nous sommes partis cinq cents ».

He then offers his opinion that the death of the preterite has been brought about by the relative ease of conjugation offered by the use of the auxiliary verbs *avoir* and *être* with a past participle: this, he asserts, has greatly simplified the past tense for all users, including foreign learners:

> *Ajouter le participe passé du verbe porteur de sens est un jeu d'enfant.* « Il est venu, il a pris » *représente une économie de conjugaison sur* « Il vint, il prit ».

The perfect is indeed much easier to produce from that point of view—overlooking for the moment the problems associated with the past participle agreement rules—than the past historic with its many inherent difficulties and irregularities. Claude illustrates his point, taking as an example the popular « Il a foutu le camp », which is within everyone's reach in conversation, whereas even the regular forms of the preterite are no longer familiar enough for people to use them with any confidence:

> « Il foutit le camp » *n'est aujourd'hui accessible qu'à une minorité de locuteurs.*

He is surprised to find, especially from the time of the *Révolution*, when the French language.was gradually being imposed on all inhabitants of the country, that the simple past was actually gaining ground in speech.   As the majority of those learning the official language had until then spoken only their own dialect, their choice of the *passé simple* in speech cannot have been a coincidence, Claude reasons. He writes:

> *Nous devons réfléchir sur cet apprentissage du français par l'ensemble de la nation, durant un siècle capital où les « émigrés de l'intérieur » ont laissé leur marque langagière dans l'auto-intégration. Au fond, le passé composé est trop simple, et le passé simple trop « composé » pour les nouveaux venus dans la glossie !*

He returns to the subject on 13 March 1997 in *Il respire encore !* and opens his *chronique* with reminiscences of the preterite, whose use has now waned in speech to such an extent that it has become alien and people no longer dare to write it, in case they make mistakes. Claude attributes its continued decline in writing, at least in part, to Albert Camus, since *L'Étranger* is used as a set text in schools and the narrative is written entirely in the *passé composé*. It should be remembered, however, that other books of Camus appearing on the syllabus, *La Peste*, for example, use the *passé simple*:

> *Albert Camus, né à Oran, écrivain spécialiste des classes terminales, doit avoir renforcé la tendance par une œuvre entièrement écrite au passé composé.*

Claude attempts to explain why the *passé simple* has acquired its perceived archaic, elevated character. Since the tense became gradually confined to the written word, over the space of two hundred years, it naturally took on an air of remote grandeur, nobility and distinction, although:

> *En réalité, le passé simple est l'inverse d'un temps aristocratique. C'est un temps du terroir, un parler de culs-terreux et de marins pêcheurs. Les langues authentiquement « populaires », au ras des marguerites comme le sont les langues régionales, l'ont toutes conservé intact dans l'usage ordinaire—les autres langues d'Europe également.*

This is indeed so, not exclusively in the case of romance languages but also in that of English and German. In both Italian and German we find that the prevalence in conversation of the one over the other varies from region to region, the simple and compound bearing the same meanings, depending on the regions, for example, the preterite is commonly found in conversation in the north of Germany, whereas in the south it is very rarely used.

Speaking from his own experience, Claude comments that in rural *occitan* the *passé simple* is still found and he quotes the example *Vengèt délum*: « Il vint lundi », where there is absolutely no trace of formality or preciosity! As a schoolgirl in the 1950s I recall hearing an extremely aged couple in Cordes-sur-Ciel (Tarn) using the simple past in conversation.   If my memory serves me correctly, it was in the statement: « Nous allâmes à l'église », the vowel *â* correctly pronounced, as by actors of *La Comédie française*, long but open—not closed, as the uninitiated might be forgiven for assuming.

When Claude mentions in this *chronique* the natural way the English use the preterite, he seems not to appreciate that in most circumstances we have no choice of tense—only one is correct in any particular situation:

> *Un pêcheur anglais dira avec un naturel semblable :* I caught some fish yesterday, « Je pris du poisson, hier ». *Ce prétérit écologique représente au contraire la parole ancienne des peuples, du temps où les hommes se mouchaient sur la manche.*

It is impossible in English to say "I have caught some fish yesterday", since "yesterday" is no longer with us: the English fisherman in question has therefore no alternative.

Claude refers to irregular verbs and the difficulties they can present, some being the conflation of two separate verbs, each with its distinctive form and history. The verb *aller* in modern French illustrates this point. During the seventeenth century people in high places often hesitated in the face of such diverse forms.   Even in a less complicated verb Vaugelas was reluctant to decide between one form and another, *il vêquit* and *il vêcut*, in which connection Claude remarks that the uneducated form ending in -*it* prevailed for a prolonged period in all conjugations, giving rise to such extraordinary forms as *l'homme « tombit »*, for *« tomba »*.

He wonders whether the *passé simple* is still a living tense. He has already expressed the opinion that the *passé composé* has taken over, largely because of the difficulty involved in knowing the correct conjugation of the former. As the users of minority regional languages and local dialects were being made to learn the national, standard language at school—*à l'école de la République*—they were instinctively drawn to the relatively easy formation of the compound tense.   Consequently, as the *passé simple* only ever appeared in writing, it began to acquire a kind of aura, *une sorte d'aura de salon,* and a decidedly upper-class character. Claude calls this phenomenon *une illusion optique* which reinforces the impression of remoteness and serves to distance it still further from its residual use.   He states that its refined aspect frightens people:

> « Nous vécûmes heureux » *épouvante, alors que* « Nous avons vécu heureux » *réjouit par la chaleur qu'une telle proposition suppose...*

The simple past, *un passé « surpassé »*, according to Claude, is now cut off from reality. How can we bring it back to life? The epigraph of this present chapter gives us Claude's clear answer: by using it!

Almost three years later, on 10 February 2000, he would return to this matter in his *Vêquit et vêcut vont en bateau*, which looks at the speed of change in the evolution of the French language. In 1647 Vaugelas had written in his *Remarques sur la langue française* that the verb *vivre* was conjugated in the past « par la plupart des gens » as follows:

> Je *vêquis*, tu *vêquis*, il *vêquit* et il *vêcut*, nous *vêquîmes*, vous *vêquîtes*, ils *vêquirent* et ils *vêcurent*.

As Vaugelas is at pains to point out:

> J'ai dit « par la plupart » à cause qu'il y en a d'autres, dont le nombre à la vérité est beaucoup moindre, qui tiennent qu'il faut le conjuguer ainsi : Je *vêquis* et je *vêcus*, tu *vêquis* et tu *vêcus*, il *vêquit* et il *vêcut*.

Vaugelas himself, not taking sides but simply recording his own observations, states his personal preference on the grounds of euphony, in one particular instance:

> J'aimerais mieux dire *il vêquit et mourut chrétiennement*, que non pas *il vêcut et mourut*, à cause de la rudesse de ces deux [mêmes] terminaisons.

Forty years later, in 1687, Thomas Corneille, the younger brother of the famous Pierre, published a new edition of the *Remarques sur la langue française*, to which he added his own commentary. To enhance the point he is making, Claude Duneton here provides as an interlude some useful historical context: in 1687 the *Roi-Soleil* was forty-nine; Molière had completed his entire *œuvre*, as had La Fontaine, La Rochefoucauld, Blaise Pascal, and all Port-Royal—in short, French classical literature had been produced in a remarkably short time. Returning to the *passé simple* of the verb *vivre*, Claude continues to set out what Thomas Corneille had to say:

> Je n'entends plus dire *vêquit*. Le prétérit de *vivre* se conjugue aujourd'hui entièrement de cette sorte : je *vêcus*, tu *vêcus*, il *vêcut*, nous *vêcûmes*, vous *vêcûtes*, ils *vêcurent*.

Claude exclaims: *Ah ! ce que c'est qu'une langue !*

The *Académie française* would confirm a few years later that *vêquit* had disappeared and « Cette façon de parler (*vêcut*) est reçue de tout le monde ». Faithful to his recurring theme, Claude questions this assertion, saying that

« un certain monde »—*le seul qui comptât*—would have been rather more
accurate, since « le monde » in question was the nobility of *la Cour*, residing
in Paris, where *l'Académie française* was at work. He comments wittily:

> *On peut être assuré que « vêquit » vécut encore longtemps chez les petites
> gens, les foules francophones des campagnes et des petites villes de la région
> francienne où l'on ignorait qu'il y eût une mutation en cours.*

The conjugation in *i* was judged archaic at the beginning of the eighteenth
century, although it was still in use among the population at large and
remained so until the Revolution and, in places, well beyond.

Is Claude right in encouraging his readers to use the tense in order to
revive it? Since the year 2000 the use of the *passé simple* has certainly not
declined further. Indeed it is still heard in the mouths of those introducing
and closing items on *France-Culture* and *France-Musique* and on the lips
of newsreaders and presenters on serious television and radio programmes.
It is not an entirely dead tense. Whether or not it can ever again become a
viable feature of the spoken language remains to be seen but it is unlikely.

Although the tense continues to be taught in French schools, and pupils
are expected not only to recognise it but to use it themselves in narrative
compositions, at least in the third person singular, many tend to conjugate
all verbs as if they belonged to the first conjugation, for example « il sorta,
il s'asseya », just as in former times their custom was to conjugate them all
as if they belonged to the second conjugation, using the popular -*it* endings
mentioned above by Claude.. When it comes to learning the imperfect
subjunctive, however, a thorough knowledge of the formation of the simple
past tense is indispensable.

Because of their close association it may be useful to see what Claude
wrote in his article *Romance subjonctive* on 26 November 2009, when he
rightly says that people sometimes find the subjunctive mood quite comical,
especially in the imperfect tense, because of its rather cumbersome endings,
-*asse*, -*assions* and -*assiez,* which with their long open *a* can sound
ludicrous and have often been exploited for this reason. Most of us will be
familiar with the examples « Ah ! fallait-il que je vous aimasse ! » and
« Ah ! fallait-il que vous me plussiez ! » which have long been used by stage
comedians. As Claude comments, even the much shorter *passé simple* can
sound ungainly in its plural forms. Alphonse Allais used to make fun of it:

> Mais de quel air froid vous reçûtes
> Tous les soins que pour vous je pris !
> De quelle cruauté vous fûtes !

It was at the end of the nineteenth century, when the standard French language was starting to usurp regional languages and dialects, that the imperfect subjunctive began to sound anachronistic and pompous, as though it had been left over from an aristocratic tongue—a noble idiom ill adapted to the *vulgum pecus* and bearing the unwelcome overtones of a past monarchy, out of place in a modern republic.

The developing chasm between the language of the people and that of the Court seemed all the greater with the combination of slang verbs and correctly conjugated endings, which produced an incongruous, ridiculous sound. As Claude wrote:

> *L'effet comique était assuré :* « Nous turbinâmes jusqu'à la nuit par crainte que nous ne bouffassions des clous ».

In the 1890s Léo Lelièvre, a Bohemian anarchist song-writer, who eventually became president of Sacem (*Société des auteurs, compositeurs et éditeurs de musique*) wrote the lyrics of a cabaret number, *Romance subjonctive*, sung to a Gaston Maquis melody:

> Fallait-il que je m'agenouillasse
> Sans que jamais je reculasse
> Pour que nous nous adorassions
> Et puis que nous nous plaquassions !

Claude is clearly enjoying the writing of this *chronique*, providing the elegant refrain in the *passé simple:*

> Dans l'amour que vous suscitâtes
> Vous fîtes germer la douleur
> Et ce jour-là vous m'épatâtes !

We can, with Claude, imagine the mirth of those at the *café-concert*, as they shouted out the chorus with all their might: « vous, mes patates ! », and then with equal gusto and enthusiasm echoed the last sound contained in the following couplet, this time in the imperfect subjunctive:

> Pour que vous m'ensorcelassiez,
> Et que vous me poignardassiez—« poignard d'acier » !

As *le passé simple* and *l'imparfait du subjonctif* have long been confined, or almost so, to the written word and thus rarely heard, their unfamiliar sounds have acquired a strangely archaic and slightly amusing character.

This being the case, anyone expecting an imminent return to the spoken language of either or both is bound, I fear, to be disappointed.

The subject of the endangered state of *le passé simple* will not go away, however. As recently as 3 January 2018, *la chroniqueuse* Alice Develey (so she describes herself) of *Le Figaro littéraire* wrote an article concerning the question: *Le passé simple est-il condamné à disparaître ?* She reported an interview she had conducted with the writer and teacher Claire Beilin-Bourgeois, who had stated:

> En réalité, ce n'est pas tant le passé simple que l'ensemble de nos conjugaisons qui est en péril.

The news that the French language syllabus had stipulated the teaching of only the third person singular and plural of the past historic had not been well received, either by those outside the teaching profession or by teachers themselves, but as the text-books are written by teachers and include the full conjugation in all persons, Beilin-Bourgeois was able to allay readers' fears:

> La plupart des enseignants n'étaient pas favorables à cette évolution, et les auteurs de manuels sont des professeurs. Nous avons donc à peu près tous eu la même ligne de conduite : suivre les instructions officielles tout en conservant ce qui nous apparaissait comme les fondamentaux.

During that same interview the important distinction between the text-book and the syllabus was emphasised, the writer assuring *Le Figaro* that the books contained everything necessary for the full conjugation of all verbs listed. Claude Duneton would have been pleased to hear what Claire Beilin-Bourgeois had to say about the difficulty of conjugating verbs and would have applauded, at least in part, her answer to the question put to her: *Le passé simple est-il trop compliqué à apprendre ou à utiliser ?*

> Le passé composé, qui est très difficile à orthographier, n'est pas plus facile à utiliser que le passé simple. En réalité, les élèves apprennent assez facilement le passé simple, et ils ne font pas plus d'erreurs qu'avec le présent, par exemple.

Admitting the virtual absence of the past historic in speech, she continues:

> C'est vrai, le passé simple appartient aujourd'hui à la langue écrite, mais il est présent dans toute la littérature patrimoniale, qui est celle qu'on lit majoritairement à l'école. Ce débat autour de la disparition du passé simple rejoint finalement celui qui entoure toutes les formes dont l'usage évolue.

Something Duneton does not seem to appreciate is that the *passé composé*, which is easy to form, thanks to the auxiliary verbs *avoir* and *être*, nevertheless brings with it all the spelling problems of grammatical agreement, which careful speakers not only write but also make audible in their speech—*les lettres que j'ai écrites*, or *mes lunettes, où est-ce que je les ai mises ?* to quote two simple examples. Furthermore, even French children sometimes conjugate the perfect tense with the wrong auxiliary verb, saying, for example, as did the little boy in the film *La Guerre des boutons*, showing equal ignorance of tense sequence: *Si j'aurais su, j'aurais pas venu, moi !*

Coming at last to the question of the imperfect subjunctive, whose form is based on the *passé simple*, Claire reminds us that Jacques Chirac was probably one of the last public speakers to have used the imperfect subjunctive. Most people never use it despite the fact that it still features in the grammar of the French language as taught in schools.

Claude Duneton would surely have advised that the survival of the imperfect subjunctive, like that of the past historic, depended on its active use—a highly unlikely scenario.

CHAPTER FOUR

VOLTAIRE, VAUGELAS, LITTRÉ AND *L'ACADÉMIE*

Si Dieu n'existait pas il faudrait l'inventer.
—Voltaire, *Épître à l'auteur du livre des Trois imposteurs*
(*Œuvres complètes de Voltaire,* éd. Louis Moland, [Paris : Garnier, 1877-1885], tome 10: 402-405)

There is a modern saying, inspired by Voltaire's famous alexandrine quoted above and parallel to it: *« Si tu n'existais pas, il faudrait t'inventer ».* Claude devotes one of his *chroniques*, first published in *Le Figaro littéraire* in early 2007 and reproduced on 28 July 2017, to this expression, which he defines as

> *une façon goguenarde de parler d'un individu au comportement bizarre, qui se fait remarquer par quelque excès de gaîté, d'avarice, de crédulité, de gentillesse même.*

Claude places this parody in the early years of the twentieth century, when *l'Église* and *l'État* were well and truly separated amid much turmoil. In 1905 France had become the first secular nation in the world and Voltaire's famous words were frequently invoked: « Si Dieu n'existait pas, il faudrait l'inventer ». The humorous *calque* was a product of the many impassioned debates of the time.

As well as providing useful background information, Claude is anxious to remind his readers that Voltaire, although certainly *anticlérical*, believed firmly in God and loathed atheists. In 1770, on the publication of d'Holbach's *Le Système de la nature*, a wholly materialistic work which shocked Europe, Voltaire had written to his friend, the lawyer and writer Bernard-Joseph Saurin, declaring the book *un péché contre nature* and seeking his friend's approval of his alexandrine, « Si Dieu n'existait pas, il faudrait l'inventer »:

> Je suis rarement content de mes vers, mais j'avoue que j'ai une tendresse de père pour celui-là.

In fact, notes Claude, there is a deep truth in these words of Voltaire, since, when we remove one god from our mind, it is only to invent another:

> *Toujours est-il que les gouailleurs de la Belle Époque détournèrent l'alexandrin brusquement mis en vedette, pour l'adapter, par effet comique, à des énergumènes.*

In 1914 René Benjamin, a subtle observer of familiar language, mentioned the parody in his *Le Palais*:

> Avec volubilité, il le redit vingt fois, l'explique trente et, renversant son buste, il a l'air d'offrir sa barbe à la déesse de l'Amitié. Celui-là, remarque quelqu'un, s'il n'existait pas il faudrait l'inventer !

In an interview with Claude, published in *L'Express* on 20 December 2004, following the publication of the first edition of *Au plaisir des mots*, the anthology of his *chroniques*, Thierry Gandillot seeks his opinion on the many fierce arguments that arise from time to time about spelling or the use of certain expressions. Voltaire again enters the picture:

> *Prenez cette interdiction de dire* « par contre » *au profit de* « en revanche ». *Le débat s'ouvre dans le Littré qui, en 1860, ne trouve rien à redire à* « par contre », *sauf que Voltaire n'aime pas cette expression ! Alors, il faut suivre Voltaire !*

Incidentally, Claude thinks that Voltaire's objection to « par contre » was simply due to its origins in commerce:

> *Moi, je pense que Voltaire n'aimait pas cette expression (qui vient du commercial* « par contre-envoi ») *parce qu'elle lui rappelait trop ses origines sociales et son grand-père drapier.*

In that same interview Claude refers to André Gide's opinion:

> *Gide s'est même fendu d'une diatribe en faveur de l'emploi de* par contre, *qui lui paraît plus approprié que* en revanche. *Surtout dans cette phrase :* « Mes frères ont été tués à la guerre. En revanche, mon mari est revenu » !

Claude had first treated this matter on 25 April 1996, in his article *Par contre, la faute à Voltaire*:

> *Oui, il est parfaitement légitime de dire et d'écrire* « par contre » ; *cette locution indispensable comporte une nuance d'opposition que ses équivalents supposés comme* « en revanche » *n'ont pas.*

On that occasion he had emphasised the neutral nature of *par contre*, contrasting it with the undeniably vengeful character of *en revanche*.

Émile Littré's *Dictionnaire de la langue française*, the acknowledged authority on all questions of vocabulary, had supported Voltaire's view and, despite stating « Cette locution peut se justifier grammaticalement », concluded: « En tout cas il convient de suivre l'opinion de Voltaire ». Thus the correct usage of the best writers of the time was dismissed, simply because Voltaire disliked it, and for the reasons of snobbery we have noted.

On 2 May 1996 in *Comme il vous plaira*, Claude introduces his *chronique* in relevant and timely fashion with reference to the old saying *En avril, ne te découvre pas d'un fil ; en mai, fais ce qu'il te plaît.* He then wonders which is right: should it be *ce qui te plaît* or would it be better to say *ce qu'il te plait ?* In 1647 Vaugelas had asked himself the same question with regard to the construction *ce qu'il vous plaira*:

> Il faut dire ainsi, et non pas *ce qui vous plaira*, et pour preuve mettons un pluriel devant et disons, *Je vous rendrai tous les honneurs qu'il vous plaira*, personne ne doute que ce soit bien parler.

Claude Duneton then refers to the subsequent comment of Vaugelas:

> *Le grammairien-conseil signalait que la phrase avec l'emploi de* qui *entraînerait* : « Je vous rendrai tous les honneurs qui vous plairont, ce qui serait ridicule »

and states that *ridicule* would not be the word we would use today.

He goes on to treat the question of *ce qui* and *ce qu'il*, quoting as examples *Savez-vous ce qui arrive ?* and *Savez-vous ce qu'il arrive ?* Both are perfectly correct, he tells us, and the two sounds, *ce qui* and *ce qu'il*, are so close in speech that there is bound to be a degree of hesitation between the two, wherever they occur. Although the constructions with the verb *arriver* are non-contentious, Claude admits that there could in fact be a subtle difference in meaning between the two, suggesting that the impersonal *ce qu'il* could lead to several possibilities, whereas *ce qui* would produce only one event.

> *On touche là, me semble-t-il, à une notion d'*aspect *du verbe—notion essentielle dans certains idiomes, comme les langues slaves, où l'on distingue dans la morphologie du verbe si l'action se produit une seule fois, par exemple, ou si elle est coutumière. Précision qui n'est soulignée en français que de manière très marginale, par le seul temps du verbe.*

Of the expression with *ce qui* our *chroniqueur* says that it refers to some defined antecedent, something clearly discernible, whereas the impersonal *ce qu'il* allows one a glimpse of a whole series of possible events. He finally returns to the May proverb, re-asserting with gentle humour that both *ce qu'il* and *ce qui* are acceptable:

> *Toutefois mon sentiment personnel est que* fais ce qui te plaît *transmet un conseil réducteur : « Habille-toi comme tu l'entends », alors que le vieux dicton s'accompagne d'une aura médiévale venue des fêtes christo-païennes du printemps ; il évoque des célébrations non seulement vestimentaires, mais une débauche de fleurs, de carols et les chants du fameux « mai entrant ». Par conséquent* fais ce qu'il te plaît *me paraît plus souple, plus ample...Après tout, le mois de mai, c'est tout un programme.*

Another longstanding debate surrounds the use of the adjective *conséquent* in the sense of *important*. On 23 June 2017 *Le Figaro* reprinted Claude's article *Les conséquences de conséquent* (2005: 184), in which he gave a thorough account of the history of this usage. Quoting from the most recent edition (1994) of the *Dictionnaire de l'Académie*, he wrote:

> *Conséquent* ne doit pas être employé dans le sens d'*important. Fort bien, mais pourquoi ?*

After all, many people—*énormément de gens*—speak of *un salaire conséquent* and of *rémunérations conséquentes*: is it really such a crime? Why is the *Académie française* so set against it? Claude wagers that the *Académie* itself does not know the true reason.

Since Claude Duneton's death the item on the website of the *Académie* has been reworded slightly and now reads as follows, though the message concerning the adjective *conséquent* remains unchanged:

> CONSÉQUENT Le 03 janvier 2013—Emplois fautifs
> *Conséquent,* comme *consécutif,* est tiré du latin *sequi,* « suivre ». Cet adjectif a donc pour sens, lorsqu'il s'applique à une personne, « qui agit avec esprit de suite », et, lorsqu'il s'applique à une chose, « qui est dans la suite logique de ». La locution adjectivale *De conséquence* signifie « qui aura des suites » et donc « d'importance ». Mais employer *Conséquent* pour « important, considérable » ou encore « gros » est un barbarisme contre lequel Littré mettait déjà en garde.

On dit	On ne dit pas
Un personnage important	*Un personnage conséquent*
Jouir d'une fortune considérable	*Jouir d'une fortune conséquente*
Un gros homme	*Un homme conséquent*

Claude finds it quite inconsistent and illogical that the *Académie*, like Furetière, should have accepted in its *Dictionnaire* of 1835 the noun *conséquence* as being the equivalent of *importance* and yet have refused—and have continued to refuse—to regard the adjective *conséquent* in the same light. Again, as we saw earlier, the reason is one of snobbery. It is with a sense of privilege—*j'ai l'honneur* ! says Claude—that he supplies the reasons for the *Académie*'s ostracism of the adjective *conséquent* in the sense of *important*. He disagrees profoundly with the *Académie*'s stance and quotes Furetière's entry from 1690 for the noun *conséquence*:

> Signifie aussi grande importance ou considération. C'est un homme de conséquence, d'un grand mérite, il a acheté une terre de conséquence, c'est-à-dire de grand prix.

Logic would dictate that the adjective should follow suit. The meaning was well established and recognised by lexicographers. How was it, then, that the language could behave so unreasonably? Where was the problem with this adjective? Claude explains that it was, again, simply one of class:

> *Eh bien, la seule difficulté réside dans le fait qu'il ne s'agissait pas d'un usage mondain, mais d'un usage mercantile, et que la bonne société qui donnait le ton et les dictionnaires n'aimait pas les commerçants !*

Wishing to illustrate how trade has always been held in disdain in France by the upper classes and wanting at the same time to amuse his readers, Claude quotes part of a brief dialogue, dating from around 1805 and, in his opinion, quite authentic, reported by the attractive young *mondaine,* the writer Sophie Gay, who was close to the Imperial Court, as she had been also to Marie-Antoinette. Madame Gay records in her *Salons Célèbres* (1831: 60-61):

> —Sais-tu bien que tu as là quelque chose de conséquent ? dit d'un air coupable [*recte* capable] un fripier ambulant à son cousin, le garçon limonadier ; j'en ai vu une épingle, dans ce goût-là, et qui a été vendue plus de 80 francs.

Although Claude chooses not to quote it, the short exchange continues:

> —Bah ! Vraiment !
> —Je te le jure. Et si tu en veux faire la preuve, tu n'as qu'à venir avec moi chez le fripier au quai des Orfèvres.

The extract from Sophie Gay's reminiscences exemplifies Claude's opinion, and he comments pointedly, with amused irony, as follows:

> *Voilà le vice rédhibitoire de* conséquent, *il est dans la bouche d'un fripier !*
> *Horreur et damnation !*

As a *fripier* is a member of the working class, very much a tradesman with his second-hand wares, the vocabulary he uses is not to be imitated by the *mondains*. Claude injects into his *chronique* a tone of mock astonishment as he provides further documentary evidence concerning the status of *conséquent*:

> *Napoléon Landais, grammairien et lexicographe, est le tout premier à annoncer en 1836 :* « Quelquefois, en style mercantile, on l'emploie pour important, considérable ». *Puis il ajoute avec une assurance stupéfiante :* « C'est en ce sens une faute grave ».

No further comment is necessary. Claude has expressed his opinion with sarcastic wit and perfect clarity: *une faute grave*, indeed.

After a brief historical detour concerning the post-revolutionary *grande bourgeoisie*, Claude, in cynical mood, imagines an improbable scenario:

> *Il ferait beau voir que la prochaine édition du Dictionnaire de l'Académie complétât ainsi sa mention :* « Conséquent ne doit pas être employé dans le sens d'important, parce que nous n'avons pas à tenir compte du langage des commerçants, fût-il utile et d'un usage ancien ». *Ma parole, c'est à vous rendre poujadiste !*

Such incomprehensible contempt for ordinary usage and such a brand of unfounded *purisme* as that responsible for banning the use of the adjective *conséquent i*n the sense of *important* can only do harm to French, in Claude's opinion, as it conveys the impression, especially to young people, that the language is inaccessible. They then, naturally, turn to English.

In a brief *chronique* reproduced in *Le Figaro* on 4 August 2017, *L'envi n'est pas l'envie,* Claude explains the etymology of these two words, which are often confused. It is not surprising to find people mistaking the one for the other, as they are homophones and almost homonyms and homographs. They both come from Latin, *l'envie* from *invidia*, meaning jealousy or hatred and subsequently desire, and *l'envi* from the verb *invitare,* which gave *envier* in Old French. The verb *envier* took on the sense of challenge to a game, as in: « À toi ! Vas-y ! T'es pas capable ! » L'envi refers to provoking one's adversary and hence implies rivalry, leading to the meaning « à qui mieux mieux ». Thus « ils chantent à l'envi » means that the one is trying to outdo the other in song. Claude remarks that it is *une jolie locution*, with a sound reminding us so strongly of *l'envie* that it has assumed a delightful ambiguity. In 1968 young people castigated the authorities *à l'envi,* but that did not prevent them from assuming authority themselves later, as our *chroniqueur* points out.

Êtes-vous matineux ? (205: 158) from 1999 was reproduced in *Le Figaro* on 10 October 2016. Readers are asked which adjective they would choose to qualify morning activities. Claude tells us that there were three possible terms in the seventeenth century: *matineux, matinal* and *matinier*. That other Claude—Claude Favre de Vaugelas—had declared:

> De ces trois, *matineux* est le meilleur. C'est lui qui est le plus en usage, et en parlant, et en escrivant, soit en prose, ou en vers.

Vaugelas goes on to say that *matinal* is not good, since some people find it old-fashioned and others consider it too modern and in any case it is not much used. As far as *matinier* is concerned, it is no longer in use, either in prose or in verse. He himself considers, however, that *matinier,* as found in « L'Estoile matinière » might well be accorded a place somewhere. Duneton adds, in parenthesis: *il s'agit de Vénus, vous le savez.* It is clear that *l'usage* has changed completely since the classical century:

> *Il y a donc eu renversement d'usage entre le siècle classique et le nôtre qui s'éteint :* matinal *demeure seul usité.* Matineux *s'est englué dans le parler dialectal, avant de disparaître avec les « patois » qui l'employaient. En 1900 le poète Gaston Couté écrivait encore : « Les p'tiots matineux sont 'jà par les ch'mins ».*

Claude wonders why this should be so. The adjective *matinal* is the most ancient, first appearing in the twelfth century as *matinel*: « Entre la messe matinel, et la grant messe ». *Matinel* changes to *matinal* in the fourteenth century, in common with other adjectives formerly ending in -*el*: « latéral, général », for example. At the same time *matineux* appears, having more or less eclipsed *matinal* by the sixteenth century, as evidenced by Nicot, who lists only *matineux* in his dictionary. Later La Fontaine would write:

> Les coqs, lui disait-il, ont beau chanter matin
> Je suis plus matineux encore.

In fact seventeenth century usage introduced a nuance between these two synonyms, as we know from the 1687 *Dictionnaire de l'Académie,* which distinguished them thus:

Matinal, qui s'est levé matin. Vous êtes bien *matinal* aujourd'hui. *Matineux*, qui est dans l'habitude de se lever matin. Il faut être plus *matineux* que vous êtes. Les femmes ne sont guère *matineuses*.

In his *Charlemagne a inventé l'école… et le français*, which appeared in the electronic edition of *Le Figaro* on 29 October 2016, Claude provides an entertaining history of pronunciation of the language, from its embryonic form found in *le Serment de Strasbourg* in 842 to the present day, admitting that it is difficult—if not impossible—to know exactly how French was spoken so long ago. He makes the assumption that the language was almost certainly pronounced as it was written. Between that far-distant ninth century and the end of the fifteenth many gradual phonetic changes had occurred. Consonants, especially the final, often disappeared in speech, and by the end of the thirteenth century many words had lost an internal *s*, as for instance *l'asne*, from the Latin *asinus*, which retained the *s* in writing, out of respect for the written word, but was pronounced [ɑn] and came to be spelt *âne*.

Turning to the seventeenth century Claude gives us a multiplicity of examples of the loss of final consonants in speech in the time of Molière and La Fontaine, quoting *bec*, which was pronounced [be]*, net* which was [ne], *tous* which was [tu] (like *toux*), and *fusil, outil* and *persil*, all of which had lost their [l].

Towards the end of the eighteenth century, and particularly during the first half of the nineteenth, many inhabitants of France learned to read. It was then that the traditional pronunciation of many words began to waver: the horse started to *hénir*, because of the spelling *hennir*, which had always been pronounced [anir]. The newly educated speakers of French were now saying [bɛk] for *bec*, [pɛrsil] for *persil*. « C'est cela que l'on appelle : l'influence de l'écrit » declares Claude, bringing his *chronique* to a close with a playful pun:

> *À propos, savez-vous que le mot* cassis *ne se prononce* cassis, *en faisant sonner l's final, que depuis très peu de temps ? Au milieu du XXe siècle, beaucoup de gens disaient encore* cassi, *à l'ancienne. D'où une plaisanterie traditionnelle des bistrots, où l'on appelait une Suze-cassis un « fond de culotte »… Parbleu, parce que le fond de culotte ne s'use qu'assis !*

Claude deals with many such phonetic changes in his article *Êtes-vous matineux* ? The more people read, the more their speech was influenced by spelling. The word *coq*, which had been pronounced [ko] by La Fontaine, acquired its sound [kɔk] through a combination of ignorance and hypercorrection. Another example of such change was found in infinitives ending in *-ir*, which had always been pronounced without the final *r*: *courir*, for instance, had been *couri* and *mourir* had been *mouri*. In similar fashion, the ending *-eur*, traditionally pronounced *eux*, now took on its modern pronunciation: *mangeur*, for example, found its final *r* sounded by *des gens comme il faut*, remarks Claude, exhibiting his predictable attitude of mild disdain.

However, it is important to note that there were no such changes in the countryside, where *coq* retained its pronunciation without the final consonant, and the turkey, *le dindon*, remained *le codinde* [kodɛ̃d] *(coq d'Inde)*. Similarly, *le faucheur* was still *le faucheux,* as he had been under Louis XIV.

The effect of such significant changes in pronunciation would be far-reaching, as the whole sound of the language gradually altered, and this created an even greater division between the academic French spoken in town and the dialectal language of the rural areas. Inevitably, as the new pronunciations appeared they almost invariably replaced those which smacked of peasant speech and ignorant *patois*. It was in this way that *matineux* was dropped by refined speakers—*les beaux parleurs*—in favour of *matinal*, a word as boastful as the cock's crow and bearing not a whiff of the land, remarks our *chroniqueur*. By the mid-nineteenth century, as Littré recorded: « *Matineux* est moins usité que *matinal* ». In order to reverse the trend and recover the sweet sound of *matineux*, Claude says one would need to get up very early indeed.

The new pronunciation of such words as *faucheur,* where the ending had formerly been sounded *-eux*, [ø], naturally had repercussions on their feminine counterparts. In his article *Le féminin compliqué* (11 November 1999) Claude refers to the difficulty of treating in equal manner the feminine and masculine forms of certain words: he takes the form *professeuse* and wonders why we find it strange and hard to accept. To find the answer we have to go back to the sources of the modern language:

> *C'est parce que la désinence* euse *n'est pas réellement le féminin de* eur, *terminaison honorable, mais bien le féminin naturel de la vieille forme en* eux, *une désinence perçue par les Français comme dialectale et dévalorisante.*

Claude reminds us that many final consonants pronounced today were formerly not sounded and acquired their new pronunciation only through the influence of the written language, as we saw earlier. Until the mid-eighteenth century, among refined speakers, the classical pronunciation [ø] in *chanteu, liseu, parleu, diseu*—still more or less intact in Quebec with *les japeux, mageux, porteux*—was the norm. The feminine of these nouns had naturally taken the form in -*euse*, by analogy with the adjectival system, which gave *fâcheux, fâcheuse*, for example. These pronunciations, which had remained unchanged in rural areas and among the unlearned, gradually became stigmatised, as they were considered dialectal and separate from the language of educated people, *le français dit « central »*.

It is surprising to note that, even in Paris, Claude tells us, the fishermen of the Seine were called *pêcheux* until the end of the nineteenth century. In the provinces, of course, *le sonneur de cloches* remained *le sonneux*. Thus, through a curious internal logic, the corresponding feminine forms in -*euse* were also considered dialectal and ignorant. Claude continues:

> *Si plusieurs termes courants ne sont pas dévalorisés—la brodeuse, la liseuse, la chanteuse, ou même la coureuse prise en bonne part, la coiffeuse—certains conservent le stigmate de leur origine « classique » : la diseuse de bonne aventure est le féminin d'un diseux, la faiseuse d'embarras vient du faiseux...*

When, however, the masculine noun in -*eur* was of learned origin (any time from the fourteenth century onwards) and there had never existed an equivalent form ending in -*eux*, a feminine in -*euse* was out of the question: as Claude says, *dans ce cas, le féminin en « euse » choque carrément*. He cleverly summarises the situation as follows:

> *La différence est parfaitement sensible avec certains mots à double usage :*
> *si le* rapporteur *est un vilain délateur qui a pu être un* rapporteux *mesquin, il a sans difficulté sa vilaine* rapporteuse *qui fait pendant. Mais, si le* rapporteur *est l'auteur d'un* rapport *(sur un projet, un budget), il souffre mal sa « rapporteuse »—on dira « Mme Édith Cauzon,* rapporteur *de la séance ».*

For the word *professeuse* to be possible, there would need to have been a masculine *professeux,* and there never was such a word. Claude invites us to imagine: « Mon mari est professeux de mathématiques à Savigny-sur-Orge ». The poor man: how he would be mocked! The modern speaker, even when completely unaware of the history, cannot accept such a form as *professeuse*: likewise *la docteuse* would refer to a *docteux*, as *l'enjoleuse* refers to *l'enjoleux*:

> *Quel féminin compliqué ! C'est pourquoi les Québécois ont inventé la* professeure—*qui clôt le bec, évidemment, aux détracteurs...*

It seems strange that the *Académie française* still refuses in 2017 to accept *la professeure*, although the word is now in current use in France, even in

Le Figaro, where on 28 August we find in a report on schools in Marseilles, entitled *Fanatisme religieux*:

> Un jour, une jeune professeure d'histoire-géographie déboule dans son bureau, fébrile.

Claude's *chronique* dated 29 May 1997 (*Puis-je ?*), reproduced in *Le Figaro* on 20 January 2017, concerns etiquette as well as language. Old linguistic forms relating to good manners are always pleasing to the ear, in his opinion, and he considers the first person singular of the verb *pouvoir*, in its inverted form, an excellent example of an agreeable sound. In recounting the history of *puis-je ?* he tells us that the form *je peux* was admitted only with difficulty and eventually became part of the language through the similarity in conjugation of the two verbs *vouloir* and *pouvoir*. This acceptance, though at first hesitant and marginal, finally came about in the latter part of the seventeenth century. Claude Favre de Vaugelas noted:

> Plusieurs disent et écrivent *je peux*, mais je sais bien que *je puis* est beaucoup mieux dit, et plus en usage.

Jean Chapelain, a founder-member of the *Académie française*, in his day the arbiter of good taste, declared himself entirely against *je peux*, which he termed « mal et toujours condamnable ». *Je peux* was still deemed incorrect by *l'Académie* in 1704: « Je *peux* pour je *puis* a été condamné et même en poésie ». Why? Claude looks at the reason given by *l'Académie* and considers it sound:

> *Elle possède, ma foi, sa dose de logique* : « C'est que le verbe pouvoir fait *que je puisse* au subjonctif, et que le subjonctif est formé ordinairement de la première personne du présent de l'indicatif ». *On ne dit pas, en effet*, que je peuve.

One could take issue with such reasoning, since the form of the present subjunctive is usually based on the third person plural of the present indicative rather than on the first person singular, though in the case of many irregular verbs (such as *aller, vouloir, savoir* and the verb under consideration here, *pouvoir*) the present subjunctive is based neither on the first person singular nor on the third person plural of the present indicative. When, during the course of the eighteenth century, the form *je peux* was finally accepted, it became firmly established in the language as a valid alternative to *je puis*, although it did not succeed entirely in ousting the older *je puis*. For example, *je peux* was never used as an inversion, *puis-je* being the only admissible form, on the grounds of euphony. As Claude says:

« Peux-je vous dire un mot ? » *est une horreur, une atroce barbarie ! Tandis que* « Puis-je vous voir un instant ?... Puis-je m'asseoir ?...» *Ah ! quelle élégance !*

The form *puis* survives also in the old negative form with *ne* alone—« Je ne *puis* vous le dire »—the *ne*, after all, being the true negative particle. Claude quotes from Corneille's *Le Cid*: « Tu le dois », says Rodrigue. « Je ne puis », replies Chimène.

To append *pas* to *je ne puis* adds nothing to the statement; *je ne puis point* is absolutely impossible, he asserts. The form *puis* belongs firmly to old-fashioned politeness: « Je ne puis venir aujourd'hui » is excellent. If one wishes to add « pas », one must use *peux*: « je ne peux pas ». When it comes to the familiar form used in ordinary conversation, it is even more the case. Claude says « je peux pas » is normal (*j'peux pas !),* but « je puis pas » *même pour les gosiers les moins délicats, ne passe pas la pomme d'Adam !*

He invites us to agree with him that « Que puis-je faire pour vous ? » conveys an entirely different impression in a shop from the rough and rather insolent Anglicism "Can I help you?" used for some time now by sales assistants, as if holding one at gun-point. He knows, of course, that they take the trouble to translate the question, but they address the customer as though they are social workers: « Je peux vous aider ?...» One is made to feel downtrodden and infirm, complains Claude. *« Comment puis-je vous être agréable ? »*—now that is what he considers correct salesmanship! In the France of the 1950s, as I recall it, the polite form in regular use by shop-assistants was: « Qu'y a-t-il pour votre service ? », an expression marked *fam.* in the 1835 dictionary of the *Académie française* and overlooked by Claude.   He adds:

> *Je suis certain que le vieux Claude—pardon ! le sire de Vaugelas— m'approuve des deux mains. Il disait justement:* « Il est de la beauté et de la richesse des langues d'avoir ces diversités ».

The demise of formerly useful vocabulary disappoints and puzzles Claude, who considers the loss of the verb *souloir* in his *chronique* republished on 27 October 2017 with the title *La lente agonie du vocabulaire français*. He regrets the disappearance of the old verb *souloir* from the modern language and wonders why such a valuable item of vocabulary should have fallen into disuse. The verb, from the Latin *solere*, meant *avoir l'habitude*, and its equivalents in Italian (*solere*) and Spanish (*soler*) are still very much alive, in the present tense, too:

> *On dira à Madrid* Solía ir a misa cada día *le plus simplement du monde, comme au présent :* Suelo tomar café *(« D'habitude je prends du café »).*

In English we have retained the verb *to be used to* in order to convey the same meaning, though it can be employed in this way only ever in the past. Claude writes:

> *En anglais, la locution* used to*, également de très grande fréquence, ne véhicule qu'une habitude passée :* He used to go to mass every morning, [...] *ou encore, plus prosaïquement,* That chair used to be in the dining-room: « *Avant, cette chaise-là était toujours dans la salle à manger* ».

In France *souloir*, such an important frequentative auxiliary verb, was gradually rendered obsolescent and had become almost extinct by the seventeenth century, though why this should have been the case is a mystery to Claude, since the verb had given good and loyal service for seven hundred years. In Old French it had been in common use, in the present tense as well as in the past. As we might anticipate, Claude provides several examples of its use from the twelfth century onwards:

> Je soloie en vo lit gésir *(XIIe), (« J'avais l'habitude de coucher dans votre lit »). Aux XVe et XVIe siècles,* souloir *était encore un verbe* « normal »—*bien qu'on ne le trouvât pas au futur :* Ainsi en icelle morte saison les gentilshommes se seulentes battre à chasser aux lièvres *(« Les gentilshommes ont coutume de se divertir en chassant le lièvre »).*

Claude includes a witty use made of *souloir* by Rabelais:

> Gargantua tient ce propos de belle logique : *Je souloys jadiz boyre tout, maintenant je n'y laisse rien (« Autrefois j'avais l'habitude de tout boire, maintenant je ne laisse rien »—dans la coupe !). Au XVIe siècle, il se conjuguait comme suit, au présent :* Je seuls, tu seuls, il seult, nous seulmes, vous seultes, ils seulent.

Scarron was still using the verb a hundred years later, in the mid-seventeenth century, although by then it existed only in the imperfect: « *En grande estime il* soulait *être* ». La Fontaine also found it useful, writing in comic mode: « *Quant à son temps... Deux parts en fit, dont il* soulait *passer l'une à dormir, et l'autre à ne rien faire* ». These two instances indicate that the verb was still understood and was probably used in conversation as late as the end of the classical period. The word then disappeared from the written language, although there were certain *archaïsants*, Chateaubriand, for instance, who occasionally produced it for effect in the nineteenth century. Then came oblivion: « À peine encore usité quelquefois », Littré recorded with regret in 1872. Claude comments:

> *Le philologue s'en chagrinait fort justement—et je suis tout à fait de son avis :* « *Souloir* est une des plus grandes pertes que la langue ait faite ; car combien *avoir coutume*, dont on est obligé de se servir, est lourd et incommode ! »

Claude wonders what can have happened during *le Grand Siècle* to cause the loss of such a useful item of vocabulary.   He first suggests its similarity in the present tense to the adjective *seul* and then considers its resemblance to the imperfect of *se soûler*, though he dismisses both possibilities:

> *Cependant, je ne crois pas à cette concurrence de l'homophonie ; surtout lorsqu'il s'agit d'un terme qui a déjà traversé tant de siècles en droite ligne du latin. Je crois plutôt que la petite notation de Vaugelas dans ses* Remarques *nous donne plus sûrement la clé de l'énigme :* « Ce mot est vieux. » *Vieux ! Tout est dit. On sent dans cette phrase le poids de l'anathème.*

He adds here, on a note of bitter resignation, that the real reason is probably contained in its very meaning: *soulait* meant « avait coutume » and thus carried within itself the seeds of its own death—it expressed tradition, and the seventeenth century hated tradition, wishing to rid itself of anything that might evoke « les vieux poètes » of the sixteenth century, whom it termed dismissively « Gaulois ». The young aristocrats and their worshippers, in a quest for modernism, despised words rooted in the language of common people and sought a new kind of Latinism, something fresh and novel. The seventeenth century, rather like our own, promoted a cult of youth, says Claude, and was *jeuniste à pertes et fracas !*

We have seen in Claude's musings on the language he loves how often he quotes the opinion of such acknowledged authorities as Vaugelas, Voltaire, Littré and the *Académie française*.   His wit, sometimes acerbic and, more often than not, sarcastic, is always in evidence and adds to the distinctive character of his writing.

In the next chapter we shall examine one of the perennial subjects treated by all *chroniqueurs du langage*—spelling—and in so doing we shall see how important a role *l'orthographe* has to play, not only in *le bon usage* but also in French humour.

CHAPTER FIVE

L'ORTHOGRAPHE

L'essentiel est de faire aimer le français par les jeunes, et quand on aime on ne compte pas vraiment les lettres !
—Claude Duneton, *La dictature de l'orthographe*, 28 April 2017, *Le Figaro.*

Maurice Druon, *Secrétaire perpétuel* of the *Académie française* at the time, addressed Michel Rocard in the presence of the *Conseil supérieur de la langue française* on the occasion of the presentation of the proposed *Rectifications de l'Orthographe* on 19 June 1990 (*Journal officiel* n° 100, 6 December 1990), declaring:

> Quand un Premier ministre se penche sur l'état de la langue française, ce qui n'arrive pas tous les jours, il met ses pas, volens nolens, dans ceux de Richelieu.

On 23 February 1994 Jacques Toubon, *ministre de la Culture*, saw his *projet de loi* adopted by the *Conseil des ministres*. This *projet*, once made law, would effectively ban the use of all jargon, foreign words and *le franglais*, and would ensure the use of French at all congresses and debates held in France. Véziane de Vezins, writing in *Le Figaro* of 25 February 1994, mentions « les marchands de hamburgers », adding « pardon, de sandwiches américains, pardon, de pains fourrés de viande ».

Any learner of the language expecting to be able to form words confidently, in accordance with established patterns, will be surprised to find that, despite such pairs as *photographe* and *photographie*, *géographe* and *géographie*, the word used to indicate spelling is *orthographe*! It is ironic that the term used in modern French to define correct writing should itself be a spelling mistake. Littré writes, in his etymological note under the entry *orthographe*:

Le grec ὀρθογράφος signifie qui écrit bien ; de ὀρθὸς, droit, et γράφειν, écrire ; l'art d'écrire correctement se disait ὀρθογραφία, qui en français donne *orthographie* […] C'est donc un usage bien fautif qui a dit *orthographe*, au lieu d'*orthographie*, surtout si l'on remarque que, dans tous les composés de γράφω, *graphe* signifie le savant, et *graphie* l'art : un *géographe* et la *géographie*, un *hydrographe* et l'*hydrographie*. Cette faute paraît appartenir au XVIᵉ siècle.

It is ironic that the word *orthographe* should itself be the result of a spelling mistake.   Until the late seventeenth century (*pace* Littré) it had the expected form *orthographie* and is thus recorded in the earliest French dictionaries: those of Robert Estienne (1549), Nicot (1613), Duez (1659) and Richelet (1680).   By 1690, however, the form *orthographe* had appeared in Furetière's dictionary—surely a misprint—and it was this erroneous spelling that the *Académie française* adopted in 1694.

With characteristic wit Sainte-Beuve, quoted by Ambroise Firmin Didot in his *Observations sur l'orthographe (ou ortografie) française* (1868: 141) wrote:

Il fallait dire *orthographie,* comme on dit […] *biographie, télégraphie, photographie,* etc.   Que dirait-on si le nomenclateur de ces derniers mots avait imaginé de les intituler la *photographe,* la *télégraphe ?* Mais commettre cette ânerie pour le mot même qui répond juste à bien écrire, convenez que c'est jouer de malheur.

If there is therefore one spelling mistake which should be corrected without delay, it is surely the monumental error of *orthographe*, whose continued acceptance casts a shadow over *le bon usage*. It is not even mentioned, however, in the *Rectifications*. It is a pity that no one noticed the error at the time and that the mistake, which had obviously been a printing error, *une coquille*, should have been allowed to survive for over three hundred years in a word signifying correct writing.

Claude's article bearing the title *La dictature de l'orthographe*, reproduced in *Le Figaro* on 28 April 2017, includes his recurring theme of how the French language—*le français central*—was imposed on the people, replacing their own regional tongues. He maintains that France is different from her neighbours, since her language, unlike other European tongues, was not allowed to evolve naturally but came about

par l'action forcée de l'école primaire entre 1880 et 1920—quarante ans, une génération d'importance capitale qui a « fait la France », intellectuelle et affective. Cette nation scellée dans un flot de sang ! De même que *l'Allemagne s'est unifiée à partir de la notion d'« aryen », la France s'est homogénéisée, dans une large mesure, par la dictature de l'orthographe.*

The French language in its present form must, however, be helped to survive, and our *chroniqueur* welcomes anything that can help to strengthen it. He recognises the vital importance of the contribution made by other French-speaking groups, such as *les Québecois* and *les Belges*, who he hopes may well prove to be the salvation of *le français de France* and prevent its final demise. He appreciates the value of the linguistic diversity that other Francophone countries bring to the language of *l'Hexagone*, with their different accents and often distinctive vocabulary:

> *[...] ces pays plus francophones de souche que la France elle-même. Nous devons intégrer cette diversité d'accents et de lexique dont jouissent les langues européennes fortes, comme l'anglais et l'espagnol.*

Those readers who are familiar with the Internet and electronic mail will have noticed in recent years the steadily increasing use in France of the Canadian term *le courriel*, the contracted form of *le courrier électronique,* which now appears to be superseding the Anglo-American *mail* and *email* (usually pronounced by the French *mèle* and *émèle*) in some circles. Claude would have been gratified to observe such a promising development.

When he refers to *la dictature* of spelling we may wonder exactly what he means. Although he readily concedes that whatever has happened in the past cannot be changed, he regrets that the symbolic unity of France, a secular republic, should be perceived as residing in a sacrosanct system of writing, and calls spelling mistakes *le nouveau péché laïc*. All qualifications gained in France—degrees, diplomas and certificates at every level and at every stage of life—have depended on one single skill: spelling. Claude continues:

> *L'orthographe fut en quelque sorte le ciment du sentiment national au même titre que le service militaire et l'anticléricalisme étatisé.*

Agreeing with his immediate predecessor at *Le Figaro*, Aristide, in this matter, he believes that any spelling reform should be minimal. The impression that we can hear Aristide speaking through him may surprise us:

> *Contrairement à ce que prônent certains linguistes trop « professionnels », il convient de réformer l'orthographe du français avec la plus grande timidité. Ce qui importe n'est pas de savoir si une modification est justifiée « scientifiquement », mais de doser les dégâts qu'elle peut produire dans l'imaginaire des francophones.*

In his strong opposition to any reform of the spelling system, Claude argues that there is no evidence to show that a substantial simplification would make the French language any easier to master. Although some scholastic publishers eventually adopted the most recent proposals for simplification in their *manuels* in time for *la rentrée des classes* of September 2016, when the changes were formally introduced in *les collèges*, the question is still being hotly debated in 2018 and *les rectifications*, initially (but no longer) approved by the *Académie française*, are being largely ignored. Rejecting the proposals, Duneton dismisses as an irrelevance the arguments concerning dyslexia, since, in his opinion, the condition is a phenomenon linked to a person's psychological state and has nothing to do with the difficulties of spelling. In fact the subtleties and complexities of French spelling are part of the charm of the written language, and he points out that no one has ever suggested simplifying the insane spelling of English in order to promote the language internationally! Furthermore, he continues, those countries which have introduced spelling reforms—Spain, Russia and Italy—have done so during periods of vibrant expansion, not in times of recession, *dans la panique d'un colmatage*.

As Claude asserts, the priority must be to teach and encourage the young to love their language. We can detect his genuine passion here, as he regards love of the French tongue as the panacea: if only children and young people were taught grammar adequately, there would be no call for spelling reform.

Earlier that same month, on 7 April 2017, *Le Figaro* had republished another of Claude's articles relating to this matter, under the heading *Mépriser la grammaire est dangereux pour le français*. The original *chronique* had been published ten years earlier, on 5 April 2007, with Claude's own title of *La grammaire et le solfège*.

We should perhaps remind ourselves here that, because of the nature of the language, there are two acknowledged categories of French spelling: *l'orthographe d'usage*, the spelling of individual lexical items as listed in a dictionary, and *l'orthographe grammaticale*, where the function of each element within the sentence determines its correct form. Unless the grammar of the clause in all its elements is fully understood, spelling mistakes are bound to occur.

It troubles our *chroniqueur* to see so many serious errors in official documents, and, although he himself knows the answer, he wonders, on behalf of his readers, how this state of affairs has come about in a society of educated people:

> *D'où vient que des gens diplômés, exerçant une fonction officielle au sein de l'appareil administratif français, parsèment leurs moindres communications de grosses fautes d'orthographe ? Ces erreurs grossières étaient jadis le lot*

des semi-illettrés, telles qu'on les trouve dans la correspondance des poilus de 14-18 écrivant à leur famille. Je crains qu'aujourd'hui ces graphies vacillantes ne soient le symptôme d'une carence plus grave.

Claude examines this serious failing, explaining that the French language is full of homophones, on account of its essentially vocalic nature, and takes as an example the sound [la], which can be the feminine definite article, as in « *la* truite », the feminine direct object pronoun, as in « il *la* voit », the musical note *la* in the tonic solfa scale, the elision of the singular direct object pronoun, masculine or feminine, with the auxiliary *avoir* as in « il *l'a* vu » or « il *l'a* vue », and can also represent the adverb *là*.   It follows that without a full understanding of the exact function of the sound [la] in a particular context one cannot be certain of its correct spelling. Wondering, again for his readers, how one becomes capable of identifying one of these five functions, distinguishing it from the other four when they all sound the same, Claude declares:

C'est simple : il faut une formation grammaticale de base, à la fois rudimentaire et solide, sinon il est impossible de faire le tri entre on l'a vu *et* on la voit.

The fact is indisputable. He then compares these sounds with their English translations, in effect a rather futile exercise, since the sounds produced by translating the five French instances of [la] fail to prove anything other than the fact that the five English renderings are five distinct words with five discrete pronunciations, which demand no particular spelling ability.

He gives three examples of elementary spelling mistakes committed by three French people from whom one would have expected better: « On ne *la* pas vu s'arrêter », from someone working in a local authority; « Que le bonheur et la santé *enveloppe* cette nouvelle année », from a mayor's office, both of these examples being in print; and a hand-written greeting from a civic dignitary, « *bonne* été ! ».   These examples, says Claude, are symptomatic of a new phenomenon found in educated people and are precisely the kind of error made by those semi-literate *poilus* we mentioned earlier, writing home during the First World War.

What has happened, then? How could anyone today write « *bonne* été » or confuse the noun *enveloppe* with the verb *envelopper* or, as is more probable, fail to know that a plural subject requires a plural verb-form, or identify which of the five [la] sounds was needed in « On ne l'a pas vu s'arrêter » ?

Claude dismisses the possibility of careless errors.   He knows only too well the reason for these astonishing mistakes:

En clair, ce sont des gens qui ont appris à lire plus ou moins globalement, comme qui dirait « au pifomètre » (« bonne été »), et n'ont jamais « fait de grammaire », du moins pas de cette grammaire au ras des pâquerettes, répétitive, lassante—passionnante aussi !—constituée par l'analyse des mots et l'analyse logique des phrases. Or cet entraînement est indispensable à l'acquisition complète de la langue française.

The perpetrators of such errors were born during the 1960s or shortly after. They had been deprived of sound teaching.   Having started their secondary education between 1971 and 1980, they were the first generation in France not to be taught to think about—and to be truly aware of—their language.

A vague understanding of French grammar is not enough, states Claude: one must know it really thoroughly, *intimement*, as one knows the tonic solfa.   If one hesitates when reading the music one cannot hope to be able to join in with the song, and it is the same when it comes to being able to write « bon été » correctly, without hesitation, and when one needs to recognise immediately the difference between the noun *enveloppe* and the verb *envelopper* as well as recognising that the verb must be plural.

Of course, he continues, those children were taught a few items of terminology here and there, information which encouraged them to think they knew more than they did, but they were never made to labour relentlessly over those basic grammatical exercises as they were over their tonic solfa notation, when they were learning to read music. It is as though they had been taught all the key signatures, all the sharps and flats and all the musical theory surrounding intervals and complicated time-signatures without ever having learnt to sing the notes on the stave. Claude is writing in all seriousness:

Ma comparaison n'est pas fantaisiste, elle est bien plus fondée qu'elle ne paraît, et bizarrement rigoureuse.

He speaks from experience, of course, having taught in schools.   He claims that during the period under discussion the emphasis was on appearing to be « intelligent » rather than on gaining fundamental knowledge. Teachers in elementary schools—people who really knew their job—were made to adopt alien methods promoted by theorists, self-proclaimed *pédagogues* and experts concerned above all with making a name for themselves *en brandissant des paradoxes*.   Senior government officials are now having to count the cost of such experimentation, says Claude.

Once again we sense his passion for the fate of his beloved French language, as he brings his *chronique* to an amusing close, with his usual wit:

*La langue française réclame une gymnastique grammaticale besogneuse—
qu'on se le dise !—régulière et tenace, sinon on confond* enveloppe *et*
enveloppe(r), la *et* là, ici *et* Issy, *et son cul avec ses chausses ! C.Q.F.D.*

Ce qu'il fallait démontrer, indeed!

His article *Mozart est là* appeared on 12 November 2009. The arguments
surrounding the proposed spelling reform, *les rectifications*, first published
in 1990, are still being expressed as vociferously as ever, even now in 2018.
In this *chronique* Claude wishes to point out a small detail he fears may
have escaped the attention of linguists, a consideration which may seem
unimportant to some, though of supreme significance in his opinion.   He is
referring to the crucial role played by traditional spelling in humour:

> *Faut-il seriner sur tous les tons que notre langue, qui a évolué très tôt dans
> le second millénaire, est formée d'un arrangement de voyelles chantantes,
> relancées par des consonnes de bas bruit ? À l'inverse de l'anglais, hérissé,
> lui, de consonnes fortes qui hachent les sons et clouent en bouche des
> voyelles plus ou moins floues, ondulantes et détendues. Il résulte de cet état
> de fait qu'énormément de mots français sont composés d'un même son
> alors qu'ils désignent des réalités sans rapport entre elles.*

He returns here to the essentially vocalic nature of French which produces
homophones such as *saint, sein* and *seing* (and, before a consonant, *cinq*),
whose meaning, when they are uttered, can be determined only by their
context, and, when written, only by their spelling, which has preserved those
very letters which are so vital to correct interpretation of the words:

> *D'où l'habitude, très tôt aussi dans les siècles, de jouer avec ces ambiguïtés
> sonores ; le jeu de mots est profondément enraciné chez les Français. « À
> quel sein se vouer ? » est une cocasserie facile qui faisait rigoler nos anciens
> libertins lettrés*

and continues to entertain not a few today.

The use of *contrepets* and *calembours* of every kind is firmly entrenched
in the French mind and has a history going back to the 1400s. Were the
traditional spelling of the language to be changed, such play on words would
no longer be possible. Pierre Burney (1967: 112) quotes the famous *homme
de petits pois* in defence of the retention of the consonant *d* in *poids*. Albert
Dauzat (1953: 46) had quoted the same example as well as: *son doit doit
être coupé, il vint vint fois* and *sans ni (nid) ni fleurs.* Claude invites his
readers to consider the many shop-signs and brand-names, both past and
present, dependent on this feature, and, speaking of *les enseignes*, writes:

> *La plupart étaient fondées sur des calembours : on cite la découpe d'un singe en bois pour signifier* Le Saint-Jean boit, *ou encore un tableau représentant le Christ arrêté au jardin des Oliviers, ce qui signifiait* Le Juste prix ! *... À mesure que les Français apprirent à lire, la vague des calembours e cessa de grandir—et cela tient uniquement aux fantaisies de notre orthographe.*

Without the vagaries of French spelling such manipulation of the language would no longer be possible.

Claude tells his readers of a recent meeting he has had with the writer Grégoire Lacroix, who is a member of the *Académie Alphonse-Allais* and worthy in the opinion of our *chroniqueur* of belonging to that other, even more illustrious body, for his defence of the French language. During their conversation the subject of spelling reform was raised, and the two found themselves in complete agreement about the role of spelling in the creation of verbal humour. Lacroix, a renowned writer of aphorisms, which he calls « *euphorismes* parce qu'ils rendent gai », had said:

> Il ne faut pas confondre *tatouage* et *peinture sur soie* : la différence réside entièrement sur un tout petit « e » fragile et muet qui porte tout le poids du sens. Aucune autre langue peut-être n'est soumise à ce point à d'aussi minces subtilités…

Leafing through one of Grégoire's books, Claude finds the drawing of a very large woman bearing the title « L'état de grasse », a grand piano drowning, dubbed « piano aqueux » and several others, including « objets dards », « la bottée du Diable », « Mes deux seins sans frontière », « poids de cent heures », « la faim des haricots » and (with reference to cosmetic surgery) « remontée de peau lisse ». Claude writes:

> *Niaiseries ? Oui, bien sûr ! En apparence seulement, car elles font pièce aux réformateurs de tout poil qui souhaiteraient voir appliquer chez nous le principe : une seule lettre, un seul son.*

Such a principle would be catastrophic. The two writers are fully aware that simplifying spelling to the point where one single sound is represented by one single letter and all ambiguity disappears would be the end of what is the very essence of French wit. Amused and impressed by Grégoire's undoubted gift, Claude quotes from a menu composed by him, where the starter appears as « veau le détour ». He closes that *chronique* with some lines of Lacroix, *Un petit pantin mécanique*, invoking Mozart's *Eine kleine Nachtmusik*:

Un petit pantin mécanique
Jouant sur son violon magique
« Petite Musique de nuit »
Est très connu en Italie.
Autrement dit : Automate, et Mozart est là.

On 18 November 2010 there appeared in the quarterly *revue* of the organisation *Défense de la langue française*, of which Claude was an esteemed member, one of his most original contributions: *L'Éloge de la dictée*. Although the article contains much that is generally recognised and acknowledged, it brings to the fore—and praises highly—a particular aspect of French dictation which is probably not appreciated by many, despite its undoubted relevance:

> *Je veux parler du rôle incantatoire de la dictée classique. Je dis bien* incantation, *car le cérémonial de la dictée en français tenait aussi du chant...*

He can speak of it in the past tense since, although dictation is still used in educational establishments, the marking system has been fundamentally revised and is now much kinder and more generous. In the past a pupil often received no marks at all for a piece of written French which nevertheless contained much that was correct. The old draconian system of entirely punitive marking was eventually deemed both discouraging and unfair. Claude is not considering at this juncture the directly grammatical aspects of the traditional dictation test but rather its solemn, ceremonial character and the intrinsic value of its literary and musical features:

> *D'abord, la lecture scandée du maître prenait un air solennel, avec cette articulation forte et précise, souvent caricaturée—*les moutonsses *de Pagnol—mais qui était de nature à provoquer la plus vive concentration dans une classe.*

Not only did the passage used for the dictation exercise have the effect of promoting concentration of the mind: the item was carefully selected, chosen expressly for its sonority and for the balance of its sentences. The extract was always of a literary nature, taken from the work of an acknowledged master of French prose. The teacher's voice would separate the passage into groups of words, reciting the clusters in turn, as though they were musical phrases, repeated and emphasised. It was this repetition, with its almost psalmodic quality, that left an indelible impression on the young minds. Claude, with his interest not only in music but also in other languages, especially English, inevitably draws comparisons:

> *Il n'en va pas ainsi pour toutes les langues : en anglais, on dicte seulement mot après mot, sans lire préalablement la phrase. Bien sûr ! il n'existe aucun accord, inutile de relier les mots entre eux puisque chacun porte sa désinence oralement ; seule compte la graphie, assez anarchique d'ailleurs.*

Of course, a dictation exercise in English has a somewhat different purpose, as it is primarily a spelling test—and Claude acknowledges the chaotic nature of English orthography—although some grammatical understanding may be required in order to distinguish such items as *there* and *their, your* and *you're* for instance:

> *En français, la difficulté—et le charme !—vient des subtilités d'accords sibyllins non prononcés. « L'école qu'elle a fréquentée », ce n'est pas* The school she went to, *proposition qui se détaille ainsi laconiquement :* Ze, skoul, chi, ouènt, tou, *sans aucune incantation possible !*

By the end of a well-conducted French dictation—chanted, intoned, *bien psalmodiée*—the average pupil knew the text almost by heart and, without being aware of it, had instinctively registered the rhythm and the beauty of the language. That daily dictation played a powerful part in a pupil's assimilation of the French language, almost as an unintended consequence, *un « effet secondaire » non prévu et non analysé par les vieux pédagogues,* Claude says. As we have seen, he regards the dictation as a piece of music:

> *Le chant clouait la langue dans l'inconscient des bambins, sans doute bien plus que l'orthographe elle-même.*

It is to its inherent cantatory, musical quality that Claude again attributes the success of the traditional dictation in teaching young people the basic rules of French grammar and spelling.

The failure of modern teaching, in his opinion, lies in the fact that intuitive, instinctive understanding has been sacrificed in favour of abstract intelligence and reasoning, which simply do not play an effective role in language acquisition. He closes his article for the *Défense de la Langue française* on a familiar note, reminding his readers of his conviction that the standard French language owes its acceptance and adoption by the people at large more to the dictation test than to anything else:

> *Je demeure persuadé que dans la période de francisation intensive par l'école, entre 1890 et 1940 en chiffres ronds, sans la dictée la langue française n'aurait pas pénétré aussi vite et aussi profondément dans les couches populaires dialectophones de notre pays.*

Claude is living in another age. He wonders, in his *chronique* of 1 February 2007, *Le mal-t-à-propos*, reproduced by *Le Figaro* on 19 May 2017 (under the heading *La faute d'orthographe ou le nivellement par le bas du français ?*), whether errors of language are a sign of a general lowering of standards. He recounts a recent experience he has had at the *gare du Nord.* As he was waiting in the queue to buy a train ticket his eye fell upon a large blue notice, proudly displayed, like an exhibit on a stand. It read:

> « Patientez ici qu'un guichet se libère ». *Bizarre formulation !* Patienter *n'est pas un verbe transitif : on ne patiente pas quelque chose, ou quelqu'un. On patiente cependant quelques minutes, mais on ne patiente pas son copain— on ne patiente pas qu'il arrive. On l'attend !*

For a moment Claude, standing in this railway station, the busiest in France with almost a million travellers of all nationalities passing through it each day, could have imagined he was in a foreign country. Who on earth would use « Patientez ici qu'un guichet se libère »? He is amazed to see the same notice at every ticket-window and asks himself: *Qui donc a écrit cette ânerie ?* He finds it strange and barely credible that in a large state enterprise such as the SNCF, among highly qualified engineers and departmental heads, there was no one capable of correcting such a gross error—after all, there is a competitive entrance examination! As he says, such a mistake as this

> *ne donne pas une haute idée du niveau d'instruction du personnel, pourtant recruté sur concours. Quelle gêne !*

Must we recognise in this particular case an example of Pierre Merle's « du français mal-t-à-propos »? Claude quotes directly from that work, where the author despairs of

> un français mal bâti, mal fagoté, perdant comme à plaisir sa grammaire, son orthographe, son légendaire sens des nuances et le reste, un français d'à-peu-près.

One might, however, argue here that the written notice « Patientez ici qu'un guichet se libère » is perfectly correct, as the verb *patienter* is being used intransitively in the place of *attendre* as a polite and tactful way of asking customers to exercise patience as they queue. It is the grammatical equivalent of « Attendez ici qu'un guichet se libère », to which expression Duneton would surely have had no objection. The *Académie française* lists the verb *patienter*: « v. intr. Prendre patience, attendre avec patience ». A few decades ago, such a notice might well have been couched in rather more formal language, most likely in the third person: « Messieurs les passagers sont priés de bien vouloir attendre ici qu'un guichet se libère ».

In general, Claude agrees with Merle that the threshold of acceptability has been markedly lowered over the past forty years.   The very idea of *une faute de français,* which, as we saw earlier, Claude regards as *le nouveau péché laïc,* has gradually disappeared, probably since the moralistic tone of the expression

> *l'a fait bannir du vocabulaire des gens avisés dans une société où la notion de morale est finalement rendue suspecte.*

Thus every *déviance* becomes normal—or even enhancing, according to some—and one word taken for another, a phenomenon which would only recently have made listeners jump out of their skin, seems no longer to trouble anyone, especially since the notion that "anything goes"—*tout est permis*—has been adopted by the public at large.

Claude recounts how a friend of his had heard a journalist on the radio announce clearly, without correcting himself, « Le témoin a déclaré sans encombre », when he had intended to use « sans ambages ».   Someone else had said, with reference to attending a ceremony, that she had come « pour le recueil » instead of « pour [se] recueillir », though, without a specific context it is impossible to pass judgment in such a case. The fact remains, however, that one could quote hundreds of instances where items of vocabulary are misused and grammatical constructions misapplied and no one even comments on them:

> *C'est ce que Pierre Merle appelle benoîtement les fautes tranquilles* ; « le garçon que je vous parle » ne fait plus réagir, pas plus que « la ville dont je suis allé ».

Although the listener will register that something is not quite right, he or she does not feel justified in intervening, reluctant in any case to seem impolite or politically incorrect; furthermore, since one has understood—or guessed—the meaning of the utterance, what does it matter? Claude writes:

> *Vive l'évolution ! s'écrient certains linguistes friands de nouveauté. Bien sûr, mais c'est de cette manière aussi qu'une langue évolue à petit feu vers sa fin.*

As he contemplates the discomfiting changes which have taken place in the language—and the general indifference to them—he attributes the blame to the educational system, which has abandoned those exercises in practical grammar which are essential for the mastery of French. He regrets that instead of *grammairiens* we now have *linguistes* who are

> *comparables à des amateurs d'émotions fortes qui regardent un enfant se noyer sans faire un geste pour lui porter secours, tant le mécanisme de la noyade—l'enfant crie, fait des gestes désordonnés—leur paraît fascinant à observer.*

Claude's opinion is that there has been a gradual deterioration in the ability of the population at large to choose correct words and expressions, mainly because educated individuals, who used to care about precision and accuracy, are now no longer interested in detail. Why is this?

> *Parce que depuis un demi-siècle on a trop abusé du charabia pseudo-scientifique, qui s'est propagé comme un chancre mou dans tous les domaines de la vie courante. L'individu de langue française subit depuis deux ou trois générations une mithridatisation au pédantisme. À force de ne comprendre qu'à moitié, il s'est empoisonné le cerveau !*

According to Claude Duneton, the erosion of standards in spoken and written French is directly attributable to the changes in teaching methods in recent generations. He bemoans the passing of the difficult dictation tests and demanding grammatical exercises of earlier times, when pupils became accustomed to hearing good literature read out to them in class and gradually absorbed—and learned to imitate—the best language and style. He would have been gratified to learn of the recent restoration of a daily dictation test in primary schools, reported by *Le Figaro* on 5 December 2017:

> Le ministre de l'Éducation a annoncé la mise en place d'une dictée quotidienne à l'école primaire

though the passages chosen would probably not meet Claude's expectations. We mentioned earlier, and quoted from, the long article Duneton had written in praise of *la dictée* for the issue of *La Défense de la langue française* dated 18 November 2010. Almost exactly nine years earlier, in November 1991, he had written an even longer article on spelling reform, *Discours aux nénuphars*, for *La Revue des Deux Mondes*. That article referred, as its title clearly suggests, to *les rectifications*, the proposed simplifications, which retained the *ph* in *éléphant* but changed *nénuphar* to *nénufar*. People in general were indignant to see their spelling and their beloved circumflex accent threatened by the state.

> *De droite et de gauche, lettrée ou inculte, la* vox populi *se mit à bramer des insultes. Le désamour suivit le désaveu. Cette crise du circonflexe ne fit que hâter, on peut le croire, la chute d'un ministère fatigué... Une sorte de pas de clerc !*

Claude's comments are unfailingly witty and never more so than in this particular article. *Le tollé général* following the publication of *les rectifications* pleases Claude and reassures him that perhaps all is not yet lost. The government and its advisers had seriously misjudged the situation, not realising that the people of France were so strongly identified with their language, sharing a name with it—*français*—that they would not countenance any state interference with its spelling.   Duneton's apt metaphor is most amusing:

> *En somme, Monsieur Rocard croyait manipuler une simple lampe de poche, alors qu'il mettait les doigts dans une armoire électrique à haute tension. On avait oublié de peindre sur la porte les zébrures d'usage, et la terrible tête de mort !*

Not only is French spelling the result of centuries of literature—and dictionaries—but it also reflects the culture of the people and has united them as a nation for over a hundred years, that is, since the standard language first began to be taught in all state schools. To be a good French citizen and to be of some worth on the employment market entailed knowing how to spell.   Duneton continues:

> *Une orthographe impeccable fut la condition absolue pour accéder à l'Administration, la loi des « cinq fautes » éliminatoires régissant tous les concours publics.*

Spelling became a state dogma. One could say that following *la séparation des Églises et de l'État* in 1905 the teaching of spelling took the place of the catechism, and the infallibility of correct writing was a substitute for doctrinal certainty. What a mistake it had been to suppose for one moment that it would be easy to rob the people of their intellectual *viatique*! Even those who had never seen a *nénuphar* were determined not to allow it to be changed to the odious *nénufar*!   Duneton had opened his article in *la Revue des Deux Mondes* in this way:

> *Le jour où l'on pourra tranquillement proposer aux Français un changement de leur orthographe, sans faire de vagues, c'est que nous aurons franchi un cap décisif de notre histoire nationale : ce jour-là le français sera mort !*

The *Académie française,* though in favour of *les Rectifications de l'Orthographe* in 1990, would eventually withdraw its support on the grounds that the changes had not been accepted by the people and had thus not entered into *l'usage.*

No matter what one may believe (or what one may have read and heard) to the contrary, the *Académie française* exists not to create but only ever to record *l'usage,* the subject of the next chapter.

CHAPTER SIX

L'USAGE OF CLAUDE DUNETON

Maurice Grevisse a, en effet, puisé à pleines mains dans les auteurs contemporains et il ajoute à chaque édition des exemples tirés de bons écrivains actuels, ceux qui, précisément, font le *bon usage* présent.
—Paul Robert, Preface to Grevisse *Le Bon Usage*, Duculot, 1980 : vii.

In his article *Le plaisir du bon usage,* which appeared on 16 September 2010, Duneton writes at length about the works of Maurice Grevisse, marking the appearance of the most recent edition of one of the late grammarian's books. He enjoys reading Grevisse and has found it hard to put down *Le français correct*:

Je reconnais que le petit avatar souple et maniable dû à la science et au doigté de Mme Lenoble-Pinson me paraît plus que sympathique : nécessaire. En tout cas, je m'y plonge et je n'en sors pas, car, on a beau connaître des choses, il est toujours amusant de confronter son savoir à celui d'autrui.

Claude knows well—and frequently refers to—the major work of Grevisse, *Le Bon Usage*, which he respects as an undoubted masterpiece of its kind. It is, however, bulky and heavy and barely portable. On the other hand, *Le français correct* is a very useful condensed version of the *magnum opus* and most welcome:

« Jamais la langue française n'a été aussi accessible » *est le slogan optimiste adopté pour la nouvelle édition du* Français correct *de Maurice Grevisse, du moins de cette refonte en raccourci du fameux* Bon Usage.

As he reads this *petit avatar souple* he discovers all kinds of intriguing information, such as the fact that many people fail to distinguish between the adjectives *cervical* and *cérébral*, a confusion which does not arise in the minds of English speakers but is understandable in French because of the noun *cerveau*. He finds in the book explanations of several strange words and expressions of interest to him (and to others, he comments) among which he identifies the counter-intuitive *solution de continuité*. Although he knows the sense of the expression—a break, a gap, a fracture—he always hesitates over it and is grateful to Mme Lenoble-Pinson for her kindly stage whisper, « solution signifie rupture ».   He jokes:

> *Et oui ! Parbleu ! qui ne se souvient que le latin* solutio *signifie* « action de délier, de dissoudre » *? Et chacun devrait avoir présent à la mémoire que* « solution de continuité » *fut un terme de chirurgie au XIVe siècle pour* « *déchirure* de la chair *», comme dans cette phrase d'Ambroise Paré:* « La solution d'unité, ou de continuité en la chair est nommée playe, en l'os fracture, et ainsi des autres ». *Le voilà, le moyen mnémotechnique :* « *La solution de continuité, c'est la plaie !* »

In more serious mood, Claude wonders what is to be said about the conjugation of verbs, which causes such difficulties for some? With the defective verb *échoir,* for instance, is it *ils échoyaient* or *ils échéaient*? (It is the latter, as he reminds us.)   This little book covers many such problematic points, but what has really impressed Claude is the very natural way in which Mme Lenoble-Pinson quotes examples of Belgian and Swiss French without making a special case for them. Of course, we may expect this treatment of Belgian usage, as she herself, like Grevisse and Goosse, is Belgian, but Swiss French is a different matter, and she treats them both equally. As Claude points out, dictionaries normally identify items of Belgian use, *les belgicismes*, and also Swiss items, as if there were something not quite right about them, whereas here, in this book, there is no such prejudice.   The impersonal verb *biser* in Belgian French is used in expressions such as *la bise souffle*: « Il gèle et il bise ».   Why should it need special treatment?   Claude, like Lenoble-Pinson, accepts the verb without comment.   And what of the famous *septante*?   How much easier would *septante*, *huitante* and *nonante* make life in France! Claude reminds us of how people have struggled from their schooldays with the arithmetical calculation required simply to make the number ninety: 4 x 20 + 10.   We find in *Le français correct*:

> *Septante, octante, nonante,* formes anciennes qui viennent directement du latin, sont en accord avec le système décimal et le bon sens.

She does not mention *huitante*, though it is more common than *octante*, which tends to belong to a rather more academic register. As Claude comments, since these forms would be understood by all French-speaking people, it really ought to be possible to write out a cheque for « nonante-trois euros », as they do in Belgium. He concludes his review of this useful *petit avatar souple* by Michèle Lenoble-Pinson, a book which he has so obviously enjoyed, with an unqualified recommendation to all his readers:

Pour l'amateur de langue soignée, ou même le chercheur de poils sur les œufs, mais aussi pour la secrétaire de base qui veut faire un tantinet de zèle, il n'y a pas mieux que ce concentré de Grevisse, accessible à tous, et tellement rassurant !

Despite all his admiration for the books of Grevisse and their updated versions, Claude Duneton prefers the expression *le bel usage* to the more commonly used *le bon usage* and defines the term at length in the anthology of his *chroniques* (2005: 142):

J'appelle donc « bel usage » l'usage du jour, celui qui règne pour l'heure, même s'il n'est qu'un feu de paille médiatique comme le fut il y a cinq ans le sauvageon. *Je ne dirai pas le « bon usage », d'abord parce qu'il est le titre illustre du Grevisse, puis parce que je m'attache à décrire ce qui est, parfois en me moquant un peu—un peu beaucoup ?—mais jamais pour « dire la loi » que je ne possède aucunement. Le « bel usage » est celui qui est dans le vent—or je tâche bien sûr d'analyser la direction de ce vent : il souffle fréquemment de l'Atlantique.*

There is surely no other grammarian or linguist who has ever thus defined *le bel usage*. Nevertheless, as this is Duneton's own definition—even if tinged with irony—we must respect it and maybe seek to establish at least some degree of affinity or *rapport* with it. It is, however, to that earlier Claude, Claude Favre de Vaugelas, that we should first turn our attention. Having been invited by Richelieu himself in 1634 to join the *Académie française* as its twenty-second member, Vaugelas was so busily engaged with the preparation of his *Remarques sur la langue française* that it was not until 1639 that he accepted the appointment. He was in demand by the *Académie* because of his acknowledged talent for observing *l'usage*, and it was thus that he became the member responsible for the preparation of the *Dictionnaire de l'Académie*. It may well have been because of his own work on his *Remarques*, published in 1647, that progress with the *Académie*'s dictionary was so slow. In the event, the *Dictionnaire* was to take all the longer to compile, since both Richelieu and Vaugelas had died by 1650.

In considering *le bon usage* or *le bel usage* we should recall what Vaugelas himself intended by the term in his *Remarques*. It is essential to recognise the distinction between *l'usage* and *le bon* (or *le bel*) *usage*, as they are not necessarily synonymous. Vaugelas states (1647: Préface I) that everyone recognises *l'usage* as « le Maistre & le Souverain des langues vivantes », and (in Préface II, 1 and 2) continues:

Pour le mieux faire entendre, il est nécessaire d'expliquer ce que c'est que cét *Usage*, dont on parle tant, & que tout le monde appelle le Roy, ou le Tyran, l'arbitre, ou le maistre des langues. [...] Il y a sans doute deux sortes *d'Usages, un bon & un mauvais.* Le mauvais se forme du plus grand nombre de personnes, qui presque en toutes choses n'est pas le meilleur, & le bon au contraire est composé non pas de la pluralité, mais de l'élite des voix.

He then delivers his famous definition of *le bon usage* (Préface II, 3):

C'est la façon de parler de la plus saine partie de la Cour, conformément à la façon d'escrire de la plus saine partie des Autheurs du temps. Quand ie dis la Cour, i'y comprens les femmes comme les hommes.

It is obvious that when Vaugelas speaks of *l'usage* in this context he has in mind *le bon usage*, as defined above, or *le bel usage*, and he asserts (Préface IV, 1):

Nous avons dit qu'il y a *un bon & un mauvais Usage* ; & i'adioute que *le bon* se divise encore en *l'Usage declaré*, et en *l'Usage douteux*. [...] *L'Usage declaré* est celuy, dont on sçait asseurément, que la plus saine partie de la Cour, & des Autheurs du temps, sont d'accord, & par consequent *le douteux* ou *l'inconnu* est celui dont on ne le sçait pas.

Vaugelas considers several cases and various ways of dealing with doubts and uncertainties, emphasising the importance of analogy.

Having made it clear in Préface VII that when he speaks of *le bon usage* he understands thereby *le bel usage*, since he makes no distinction between the two, in Préface VIII he attempts to dispel the widely held fallacy that *le peuple* dictates *l'usage*. In so doing he attributes this misapprehension to a simple ignorance of the Latin language, since some have taken the French word *peuple* as the translation of the noun *populus*, whereas its true equivalent is *plebs*. Vaugelas explains that *populus Romanus* includes « les Patriciens & l'Ordre des Chevaliers » as well as the ordinary population, stating :

Selon nous, le peuple n'est le maistre que du mauvais Usage, & le bon Usage est le maistre de notre langue.

More than three centuries after Vaugelas, Philippe de Saint Robert would provide a similarly useful distinction in his *Lettre ouverte à ceux qui en perdent leur français* (1986: 179):

Il convient ici de ne pas confondre ce que les linguistes sont convenus d'appeler *l'usage*, qui correspond au laisser-aller du moment élevé au rang de référence, avec la conception plus normative et plus académique du *bon usage*, qui en est à peu près l'opposé.

There tends to be divergence of opinion among linguists and grammarians concerning the concept of *l'usage*, linguists generally taking the language used by the majority of the people as the accepted norm, the true language, whereas most grammarians interpret *l'usage* as *le bon usage*, defining it as the language used by careful speakers and writers. With this fundamental disagreement in interpretation there are corresponding differences in attitude and approach, and we should probably judge Claude Duneton's definition of *le bel usage* in this context. Does he call *bel usage* the *laisser-aller du moment*? Such might well be the case, were it not for his sarcasm and ironic humour.

As we have observed, our *chroniqueur* likes to return wherever possible to the source of the word or phrase under discussion, and his study of the history of the item sometimes justifies its new use, as is the case when the adjective *riche* is applied to food, a usage now current in France:

> *On entend de plus en plus souvent cet anglicisme qui consiste à dire d'un aliment, d'un mets, qu'ils sont* riches, *au lieu de nourrissants.*

We could take issue with him here, since he seems not to appreciate that *rich* in English does not usually imply *nourishing*. When used of elements of foodstuffs—vitamins and minerals, for example—*rich* indicates an abundance: it is held, for instance, that spinach is *rich* in vitamins K, A and B complex as well as in magnesium, iron and copper. The adjective *rich*, when applied in English to a dish, however, indicates more often than not that the food is delicious (rather than nutritious), being full of cream, butter, eggs and fat, and will probably give one indigestion.

Then, quoting a more appropriate parallel, « Votre cassoulet est excellent, mais beaucoup trop *riche* pour moi », Claude makes an amusing comment about *cet anglicisme*, one of those which have been blown in from across the Atlantic:

> *Il n'est pourtant pas semé de perles—tout simplement les gens vont en Amérique, là-bas on leur parle de* rich food, *ils trouvent au retour que ça fait* riche *de s'exprimer ainsi et vous bassinent de* « nourriture riche » *à tous les repas !*

The explanation Claude then gives his readers concerns the etymology of the word in question, and here he comes into his own. He informs us that the French adjective *riche* comes originally from the Frankish *rîki*, meaning *powerful*, from which emerged the German adjective *reich* and the English *rich*. Of the French adjective *riche* he writes:

> *C'est en effet « la force, la puissance » qu'évoque le mot* riche *dans les deux premiers siècles de notre littérature médiévale. Ainsi dans le* Guillaume d'Angleterre *de Chrétien de Troyes, vers 1165, le roi se lamente de la perte de son petit enfant qu'un méchant loup lui a ravi : « Ha ! loup, pure bête haïe/Moult as or fait* riche *envaïe... »*

Incidentally, according to Duneton, it is fairly often the case that the English word has remained more faithful than the French to the original meaning. He provides a further instance of the use of the French adjective in « riches murs » in the context of a castle, where the fortified walls are strong, thick and solid, capable of withstanding a « riche siège ». One also finds the expression « riche cœur » in the sense of « fort courage ».

Returning to Claude's passing reference to a new use of the word *sauvageon* (2005: 169 and his original *chronique* entitled *L'âpreté des fruits du sauvageon* of 1 April 1999)—a usage which appeared at the very end of the twentieth century and provided an excellent example of that flash-in-the-pan word or expression that appears out of the blue only to disappear as promptly as it arrived—we observe once again how he supplies the history of the term, though he would surely not place this new use of *sauvageon* in the category of *le bel usage*: or would he? He informs us that the only definition of *sauvageon* given by Littré in 1872 was the arboricultural term:

> Arbre venu spontanément dans les bois, dans les haies, de pépins ou de noyaux de fruits sauvages.

Le Grand Robert (1966), however, lists also a figurative meaning, approximating to the one under discussion:

> Par attraction de *sauvage*, enfant qui a poussé pour ainsi dire tout seul comme un petit sauvage.

The latter definition brings us much closer to Duneton's new-fangled, short-lived meaning, introduced by Jean-Pierre Chevènement when *ministre de l'Intérieur*, on 10 January 1999. Chevènement was reported in *Libération* on 12 January as having used the term *les sauvageons* two days earlier on TF1 with reference to *les mineurs multirécidivistes*. Although the Minister was criticised by many for his use of the word in this sense, since it was regarded as stigmatising and was perceived as excluding a set of young people with problems, the term became popular overnight, thanks to the media. Claude provides his own definition:

> *On pourrait dire que les* sauvageons *sont maintenant de « jeunes garçons qui vivent en groupes dans les banlieues, enfants ou adolescents, émigrés [sic] ou non, qui se livrent pour se distraire à des actes répréhensibles, tels que l'incendie de voitures, ou la destruction volontaire de locaux voués au commerce ».*

He comments that this would appear to be a new sociological category, quite distinct from the hooligans and vandals of the 1970s, different, too, from the adult protesters of May 1968 and very far removed from *les blousons noirs* of the 1950s and 1960s. Claude says that *les « sauvageons » sont une nouvelle classe de délinquants* and he wonders whether the term will grow and intensify. He thought by the year 2005 that the expression had been only transient, having already fallen into disuse: it was to return, however.

From his article *Citoyens, citoyennes !* (2005: 166) we learn that these nouns have now become adjectives, though not for the first time in the history of the French language. In the eighteenth century the citizens of Paris who were working on the 1771 edition of the *Dictionnaire de Trévoux* had noted cautiously that « Quelques écrivains ont fait ce mot adjectif ». At the time, that was all they said, but the adjectival use became more and more prevalent during the period of the *Révolution*, where *citoyen* and *citoyenne* officially replaced *monsieur* and *madame*. So common did this usage become, Claude informs us, that the 1835 edition of the *Dictionnaire de l'Académie française* had the following entry: « Citoyen se prend quelquefois adjectivement dans le sens de Bon citoyen [*sic* pour la majuscule, adds our *chroniqueur*]. Un ministre citoyen, un roi citoyen (*et, en 1835, il était tout frais émoulu, ce roi-là,* comments Claude in jocular mode), un soldat citoyen ». The next year, Napoléon Landais confirmed the usage and, finally, Littré mentioned it in 1863 with the meaning « Dévoué aux intérêts de son pays », citing « Ma muse citoyenne ». Claude reports that twentieth-century works of reference did not include the adjectival use, since it had become obsolete within a century.

On 16 October 1997, in *La tendresse du gigot,* Claude uses the term *bel usage* as we would normally expect to find it and, as usual, provides an absorbing history of a lexical item, on this occasion *la tendresse*. He tells us that *certaines personnes* are reluctant to use it when referring to meat, fearing that the noun will become debased or trivialised if so employed:

Elles ne peuvent accepter, par exemple, que le prix du gigot soit à la mesure de sa tendresse... D'aucuns s'élèvent même vertueusement contre un tel usage qui leur paraît un lèse-cœur !

Such people maintain that the only correct term to be used of meat is *la tendreté*—and the same applies not only to the plaster on the wall but also to both poplar and elder wood. Claude agrees with their criticism, affirming that they are quite right...

Mais la logique n'est pas ce qui commande aux sentiments, n'est-ce pas ? En réalité, soyons prudents : il règne un grand flou dans la carte du « tendre »

His allusion to *la carte du tendre* and thus to *les précieuses* is both witty and pertinent, since his treatment of *tendresse* and *tendreté* is precisely the kind of discussion held in the seventeenth-century *salons littéraires* of *l'Hôtel de Rambouillet.* Claude is in his element, as he now engages in etymology. Having taken us through the history of the adjective *tendre*, from its Latin origin, *tener*, through the occurrence of *un cœur tendre*, found in *la Chanson de Roland*, to its use in the twelfth century by *le Châtelain de Couci*, he informs us that:

Le substantif est alors tendreur—*eh oui ! sous la forme* tendror—*un mot qui a mal supporté le voyage du temps : il est encore là, tapi, prêt à servir, mais il est « inusité » pour* Littré, *tandis que le* Robert *l'a carrément abandonné.*

In fact the noun *tendresse* arrives relatively late, at the beginning of the fourteenth century—*ce siècle si dur, si noir !* Like *tendreur*, however, it continues to bear more than one meaning. The noun *tendresse* can indicate anything that is not old or hard, such as *la jeunesse*—indeed, in the beginning it was sometimes used for *l'enfance*—as well as « la sensibilité exquise pour les choses morales » and « les sentiments tendres d'amitié, d'affection » and, adds Claude, *l'amour, toujours !...* He continues:

En même temps paraît le mot tendreté *(dans* Le Roy Modus, *livre de la chasse), avec application aux choses concrètes : les blés, les viandes.*

During the sixteenth century the word was *en assez bel usage*, Claude tells us, again using the term *bel usage* with a less idiosyncratic meaning than the definition quoted earlier. Perhaps he was writing tongue-in-cheek, as is his wont, though he certainly seems to regard *le bel usage* as reflecting a passing fancy, a fad, a whim, something temporary rather than permanent. Referring to the sixteenth century, he says:

Ambroise Paré parle de la tendreté *des os. Olivier de Serres de la* tendreté *des racines. Il semble que c'était un pas en avant vers la précision, un élément de rationalisation intéressant—et mes bougons de commencer à se réjouir : « Ah ! vous voyez bien ! Nous avons raison ! » Oui, mais...*

Claude explains that *les classiques* soon put an end to this tendency, since Vaugelas, the all-powerful oracle of *l'Hôtel de Rambouillet,* pitted himself strongly against such use of *la tendreté*:

Il déclara—et cela fit jurisprudence—entre le pluriel de quelqu'un *et l'accusatif après* sentir *: «* Tendreté *ne vaut rien,* tendreur *encore moins ; il faut dire* tendresse *». Diable ! c'était un faux espoir... Le moyen, je vous prie, d'aller contre Vaugelas ?...*

As we have seen before, the word of Vaugelas tended to reign supreme. It is said that in Paris at the beginning of the nineteenth century, sellers of vegetables used to cry out in the street, at the top of their voice:

Mes artichauts !... Mes beaux artichauts !.... Toute la tendresse, toute la verduresse !

In summary, Claude advises his readers to accept the possibility that a hostess may well be right when she speaks of *la tendresse du gigot* !

Does he deal with *le bel usage* in his *Un peu beaucoup,* the title of his *chronique* published on 17 August 1995? Here he writes about the habit acquired by many people of inserting *un peu* into every statement they make, regardless of meaning and relevance. This common speech habit he calls *un tic de langage*, remarking wittily that it crops up with *une fréquence « un peu » déconcertante.* He quotes several amusing examples:

Quelqu'un dira : « J'ai un peu de mal avec la banque *», ce qui signifie qu'il a des soucis d'argent aigus. «* Je suis un peu pressé *» veut dire «* Je n'ai pas une seconde à vous consacrer *».*

Claude wonders whether this continual use of *un peu* could indicate a fear of excess. Perhaps people have become wary of stating anything other than a slight tendency:

Le cimetière n'est plus triste, mais « un peu triste *», les vacances ne sont pas chères, mais «* un peu chères *», le ciel «* un peu couvert *», le dimanche «* un peu long *», le discours «* un peu ennuyeux *»—nous avons même inventé le comble avec la formule «* un peu beaucoup ! *»*

Have people become unwilling or unable to state their opinion? This question leads him to consider how things have changed since the early years of the twentieth century, when people knew right from wrong, when they could distinguish salt from sugar, heat from cold, male from female and the lovely from the ugly. Claude continues in this vein and we recognise the man we have encountered before. He is the man weary of the age in which he lives. In his reminiscences he evokes a time he considers lost forever, referring to *l'homme du début du siècle*, who was so different from his late-twentieth-century counterpart:

> *Il connaissait Dieu, redoutait l'enfer, haïssait l'Allemagne, aimait le bœuf miroton, les expositions coloniales, et les chansons du café-concert. Le président s'appelait Poincaré, il avait le verbe rond.*

Here we must ask ourselves whether Claude Duneton is being entirely serious: is he making these challenging points in order to strengthen his argument or is he being ironic? The fact that our *chroniqueur* believed in God prompts us to accept what follows, though we may question his stark statement about the hatred of Germany, though on one level it is certainly the case, as it was the First World War that brought so much suffering and death to many young Frenchmen, contemporaries of his *corrézien* father, on whose behalf he would write *Le Monument*, his *roman vrai*, in 2005. People in the early years of the twentieth century used to enjoy the homely, tasty *bœuf miroton*, typically made from left-overs, and they loved going to the cabaret, where they would join heartily in the singing. Would he have supported the President's politics or does he simply admire Raymond Poincaré for his straightforwardness and frank speaking? We should take the paragraph seriously, as it shows the writer thinking aloud, drawing an honest comparison between the France in which he was writing in 1995, and the France of the second decade of the twentieth century.

A little over two years later, on 13 November 1997, Claude refers again, in a very similar article, *Un peu sur les bords* (reproduced in *Le Figaro en ligne* on 30 June 2017, two decades later), to another *tic de langage*: there are people who unfailingly include in every statement they utter the expression *sur les bords*. He suggests, in full metaphoric flow, that we should not make fun of them:

> *Il s'agit d'une de ces bulles verbeuses qui montent crever au jour du fond marécageux de nos consciences repues d'Occidentaux aux mœurs émoussées...*

We glimpse in his writing a hint of that world-weariness, *un mal du siècle moderne* that we have detected before: the blunted morality of our age affects him, though without actually depressing him, since he accepts it with ironic resignation.

He regards *sur les bords* as a *formule de modération*, indicating a tendency, rather as one used to refer to « un penchant » in former times:

> « Tu ne serais pas un peu alcoolique sur les bords ? » veut dire : « Tu bois beaucoup, c'est inquiétant ». *Notez que la formulation est doublement nuancée, car elle implique toujours* un peu. *On ne dit pas :* « Il est fou sur les bords », *qui aurait une allure trop concrète—quels bords ?—partant, trop incongrue.*

He thus supplies an amusing example of this particular *tic langagier* with fitting commentary.   In fact, Claude says, *sur les bords* is a way of reducing the sense of *un peu:* « Il est un peu malade » signifies « Il ne va pas très bien, il a un début de grippe », for example, whereas « Il est un peu malade sur les bords » removes the reality of a true illness and produces something vague and meaningless. He considers that *un peu sur les bords*, being *une double modération,* should be placed in the same linguistic category as *la double négation* and offers the following in jocular mood:

> *Si vous dites de quelqu'un* « Il est un peu salaud, ce type », *cela indique qu'il l'est beaucoup. Tandis que :* « Il est un peu salaud sur les bords » *exprime un état de vilenie intermittente, une hypocrisie tempérée, une forme pas totalement nette de saloperie larvée... Ah ! la médisance !*

Claude considers *les bords* highly symbolic of our modern ways of thinking. These days we are far less interested in the heart of things but concentrate rather on the peripherals.   Our mind is set on the marginal.   He mentions the current mathematical research into *la logique floue*, which concerns the mathematics of boundaries and limits, *là où le oui a la valeur de « oui et non ».*   The image depicting this research is the edge of a cloud, the imprecise area, where one cannot be sure whether it is still a cloud or has become blue sky:

> *Pourquoi en est-il ainsi ? Probablement parce que le cœur des choses nous semble exploré, avec ses limites, ses frontières, comme la terre et sa rondeur ; les explorateurs sont passés à la Lune, à Mars à présent. Les lois du blanc et du noir ont dû être remodelées, relativisées.*

Our reasoning is similarly affected: *bonnet blanc* is no longer in any way the same as *blanc bonnet*. Claude exclaims: « *Nuances partout !* » The square is now drawn in the circle, but the circle is no more than an extreme example of a regular polygon.   It is the perimeter that matters now— *l'anneau, la couronne.* Accordingly, no one cares any longer about city centres—those of Paris, Lyons or Marseilles—but only about the suburbs. Using vivid language, Claude writes:

> *En revanche, leurs banlieues font couler des wagons-citernes de salive et d'encre. Il en va de même pour le citoyen tout rond, besogneux, le père attentif, respectueux des lois, et pour ainsi dire « central »—il ne fait pas audience. Tandis que le toxicomane intrigue, le parent abusif fait dresser l'oreille, le pédophile surprend, le hideux fascine, le filou fait un malheur ! Ce sont des vedettes du pourtour, portées très haut sur l'affiche.*

Here Claude has departed from the main object of his *chronique,* launching into the realms of philosophy and sociology.   He adds that the expression first appeared in the 1940s—and that was a period of turmoil—and not only *sur les bords.*

It is inevitable that the world of *l'ordinateur* and *l'informatique* should feature in any consideration of *le bel usage,* at least in Claude's sense of the term.   He is incredulous and astounded to hear the claim that computers have not affected people's writing at all. He smiles.

His first comment concerns reading on screen, which is difficult and quite different from reading a book or anything written on a sheet of paper— *le papier repose l'œil, l'écran le fatigue.*   The on-screen text we read demands far greater attention and concentration than the traditional written word, and Claude likens the effort we have to make in order to read it to that involved in driving a car when we have the sun in our eyes, dazzling our vision. Furthermore, since long sentences, running to several lines, are far harder to read on screen, writers who use word-processors tend to shorten and simplify their sentences. Claude suggests we try reading a few pages of Proust on our computer screens. He writes:

> *Les phrases courtes rassurent. À l'inverse, des phrases complexes, truffées d'incidentes, qui caracolent d'une ligne à l'autre, affolent. Elles semblent échapper à la surveillance du scripteur et prendre seules la clef de champs incontrôlés. Les phrases longues paraissent suspectes, inquiétantes, peut-être minées. Et tout cela se passe dans l'esprit du pianoteur sans qu'il en ait conscience, bien entendu.*

He wonders if that explains how he can always detect immediately whether a novel has been typed or whether it has been word-processed on a computer. The old-fashioned typewriter, in his opinion, is completely different from a computer, as it gives a *« texte placide », doux et calme,* almost like handwriting. He adds, in parenthesis, for the sake of the typesetters at the newspaper: *phrase écrite à dessein avec un stylo à bille.* According to our *chroniqueur,* word-processed text is readily identifiable by its short sentences, most of which have fewer than twenty words and many of which have no verbs. He states, with a delightful touch of irony:

> *Je n'ai rien contre ; je constate simplement que ce n'est pas ainsi qu'opérait Chateaubriand avec sa plume d'oie.*

His humour continues. Claude asserts that the equipment used in writing influences the text in the same way as agricultural machinery affects the land being ploughed:

> *J'affirme que l'outil influe sur l'écriture, comme la charrue à cinq socs sur les labours.*

In the long run, he says, the computer profoundly alters the *couleur* of our writing.

He had recently read an article in the Belgian publication, *Francophonie vivante*, from which he quotes:

> Dans les grandes entreprises les formateurs recommandent, en communication écrite, de ne pas dépasser 25 mots par phrase dans une lettre ou un courrier (parfois moins encore), *et 10 à 14 mots par phrase de courriel.*

Those are Claude's italics. He is delighted to be able to show his readers that he is not the only one to hold such opinions, adding that the average length of a sentence in novels of the younger generation is fourteen words.

Another side-effect of the word-processor is to produce incorrect sentences. Inaccurate word-counts abound: they may be either inflated or understated because of errors arising from the "copy-and-paste" function. He reports having read in the quarterly review, *Lettre du Chemin des Dames*, the following notice: « Le décès d'Albert Balasse n'avait été pu être officialisé que le 31 décembre 1919 [*sic*] ». Claude explains:

> Ce « n'avait été pu être » *proviens immanquablement du coupé-collé d'une* « n'avait été officialisé » *avec la rectification* « pu être » ; « été » *est resté en scorie dans la refonte, aucun correcteur ne s'en est aperçu, ce qui aurait été à coup sûr le cas dans un* « texte placide ».

From that same notice he quotes a further example of the depressingly common textual errors arising from careless copy-and-paste techniques, stock phrases being inserted without due care, willy-nilly, whether or not they make any sense or belong logically in the context:

> Dans le cimetière ils avaient inscrire sur la pierre du caveau familial « À la mémoire d'Albert Balasse ».

The past participle *fait* had obviously disappeared when the construction *faire mettre* was replaced with *inscrire*, and no one had noticed the mistake when checking the on-screen text.   This type of serious grammatical error is becoming more and more prevalent in all types of publication:

> *Mais on ferme les yeux, si j'ose dire, laissant au lecteur le soin de restituer mentalement le sens, parce que l'ordinateur a tous les droits—il est notre guide à présent, notre soutien, on lui pardonne tout. Alors qu'on passait naguère un savon sérieux à un typographe qui aurait laissé des bévues pareilles dans sa page.   Autre temps, autres mœurs...*

It is on a note of bitter irony that Claude ends this *chronique*, dedicating it to Albert Balasse, the *poilu* who gave his life on 5 May 1917—not 1919—*au Moulin de Laffaux*, so that we might one day have wonderful computers at our disposal.

CHAPTER SEVEN

LES MOTS—
ET QUELQUES BIZARRERIES

Les mots ne sont immuables, ni dans leur orthographe, ni dans leur forme, ni dans leurs sens, ni dans leur emploi.
—Émile Littré, *Dictionnaire de la langue française*, Hachette, 1873
Préface : X. Conclusion.

Claude is delighted, and perhaps a little surprised, when the *Académie* decides to recognise certain items of regional vocabulary: *L'Académie s'ouvre au français « décentré »*, he announces in his article *Des jolis mots* (2005: 156). These words now recognised by *la société du quai Conti* do not belong to the standard, central language of the « haute bourgeoisie parisienne cultivée », *siege traditionnel du bon usage*.

On 4 June 2009 Duneton writes a review, *L'homme des listes*, of the recently published *Dictionnaire amoureux des langues* by the celebrated linguist, Claude Hagège, stating at the beginning of his *chronique* that he does not share the current enthusiasm for presenting so much subject matter in the form of dictionaries, though he understands the possible commercial reasons for this fashion, since terms denoting works of reference lend an air of seriousness, authority and authenticity to the publication, from the outside at least—« c'est vrai puisque c'est dans le dictionnaire ».

Although our *chroniqueur* admires the immense knowledge contained in the work, he wonders for whom the dictionary is intended. It consists essentially of bite-sized items listed in alphabetical order. Although he finds the dictionary exciting in places, he finds it also disconcerting and disappointing, as the quality is so uneven:

Il constitue un mélange d'érudition très pointue, capricieuse et rare, et de banalités sur les « prodiges d'imagination que l'esprit humain enfouit dans le discours sur le monde »—à propos des façons de dire « il pleut » en russe, hongrois, hébreu, turc, albanais, chinois, japonais, thaï. Et en arabe : « le ciel répand la pluie », ce qui est joli. La masse d'informations que cet homme est capable de dévider est effarante ; il me fait l'effet d'un Google à lui tout seul.

Inevitably, some entries consist simply of items of vocabulary in different languages; others, such as the article on translation, arouse a lively interest and provide a depth of information; yet others do not go far enough to satisfy the serious reader. The chapter on *politesse*, for instance, gives an all-too-brief review of expressions of deference used around the world and gives somewhat perfunctory advice on when to address people formally and when informally. This section deserved a book to itself rather than the over-academic, brief outline. Hagège indulges his love of languages, using Chinese, Japanese, Turkish and Arabic as if they were one universal mother-tongue. It is unsatisfactory, as the reader is left in a fog of allusions. What he says of this section applies also to the chapter on the names of languages, where the author seems to be in too great a hurry to jump from Greece to Bolivia and from Arizona to Russia. Claude Duneton says of Claude Hagège:

> *On dirait qu'il murmure : « Je ne m'étends pas davantage, je suis horriblement pressé. J'écris un dictionnaire, là. Je vous en prie, n'insistez pas ! »… C'est dommage.*

Hagège reports *en passant* that a Turkish law of 1983 forbids the use of any languages other than those recognised by the state, in order, it would seem, to exclude Kurdish. Our *chroniqueur* comments that such a law may seem harsh, yet he reminds his readers that it had been only a little over a century ago that the Third Republic had forbidden the use of all regional languages in order to combat « les opinions » traditionally rooted in the speakers of the various *patois*:

> *les convictions religieuses, en particulier : en 1904, un curé de basse Bretagne fut cassé par le ministère des Cultes parce qu'il avait été surpris à enseigner le catéchisme en breton ! En vérité, ces Turcs outrecuidants ne font que répéter ce que firent si bien les Français au siècle précédent.*

He finds under *Orthographe* (between *Opéra* and *Ouolof*), a long list of English words, illustrating how English spelling has no rules. Hagège refers to French spelling and the *Rapport du Conseil supérieur* dated 6 December 1990, setting out the planned changes to the spelling system, which finally saw the light of day in September 2016, although most people have so far ignored the recommendations, as our *chroniqueur* knew would be the case. Hagège seems not to understand why people are so resistant to changes in the spelling of their language. As we know, Claude Duneton objects strongly to the proposed *Rectifications*, making a fervent plea:

> *Quand donc les linguistes de haut babil s'inquiéteront-ils de savoir réellement ce que cache—ou traduit—le refus des Français de voir voltiger les graphies ? Quand une analyse sérieuse prendra-t-elle en compte l'histoire particulière de cette langue imposée par la politique, au détriment des langues mères de l'Hexagone, et qui fit de savants orphelins ?*

Claude Duneton never misses an opportunity to remind his readers of how the modern French language had come into being. The shops are full of books about the French language, a reflection, in his opinion, of the current state of affairs. He writes:

> *J'attends que de puissants cerveaux comme celui de Monsieur Hagège s'attaquent à la question autrement que par le persiflage.*

He states in his article, *Le délitement de la langue française est dangereux*, republished by *Le Figaro* on 20 October 2017, that new books are appearing all the time and the French as a nation are deeply concerned, not only about the degradation of their language but also about the values of a society which is showing signs of instability and appears to be taking a completely new direction. It is rather like a man lost in the forest at night, he says, whistling in the dark to give himself courage.

On this occasion Claude's *chronique*, which first appeared on 21 January 2010, is the review of a book he has just read, *La Langue française au défi*, by François Taillandier, in which the author discusses the present state of concern about the language and cautiously—for, says Claude, we must not be seen to be retrograde!—comments on the collapse of the classical culture which justified the nation historically. Taillandier says that the French are fearful because the very foundation of their *francité*—in other words, the essence of their "Frenchness", which is their language—is no longer a reassuring, solid structure unifying the nation; instead, knowledge of the language has vanished, seemingly with official consent, amid the noise and clamour of egalitarianism.

It has all to do with our modern way of life and how everything has changed so swiftly and so profoundly: Claude knows that it is impossible to change suddenly from being a society marked by bells, school and the local *bistrot* to a world of supermarkets, television, decentralisation and suburban sprawl. Regarding the parlous state of the French language as a consequence of the abandonment of good literature in favour of the Internet, Claude comments:

> *Oh, oh ! dira le progressiste de métier, c'est la joyeuse évolution qui se manifeste ainsi. Qu'avons-nous besoin de ces vieux textes classiques aussi inadaptés à notre présent d'Internet que les vieilles lunes ?*

He shows that he has little time for linguistic innovators:

> *Le progressiste, qui ne craint ni la mort ni le ridicule, oublie toujours que*
> *son temps de vie, le temps du moment, est un instant précaire…*

and develops this theme, reminding his readers that the various dialects of France had become a language as early as the thirteenth century because they had already experienced two hundred years of a flourishing literature: Rutebeuf and Jean de Meung had been the heroes of a growing culture. The French language has never failed to be enriched by its literature, and to deprive the new generation of the writings of the past—and here he quotes Taillandier—is to

> incarcérer ceux qui viendront dans l'à-plat du présent, les persuader qu'en fin
> de compte leur monde se suffit à lui-même.

Claude sees such a policy as driving the young back to an age where there was yet no culture.

Given the overall laxism, which, as he reminds us, is both created and sustained by a select few, whose working language is actually English, Monsieur Taillandier's little book, from which Claude quotes again, reminds us of fairly elementary principles which would seem to be disappearing while utopians await a nirvana leading to eventual oblivion:

> Une société humaine digne de ce nom est précisément faite de règles parfois
> incommodes qui peuvent paraître inutiles et que l'on observe cependant.
> […] Laisser se déstructurer la langue au nom du pragmatisme ou de la
> facilité revient à déstructurer l'individu.

To establish the truth of this sad fact, Claude says, one has only to glance around. We can appreciate how closely he identifies with the opinions of Taillandier, who rails against those destructive ideologies which were all the rage in the late twentieth century: « *l'hallucinante énormité* » and « *La langue est fasciste* » of Roland Barthes.

Several years earlier, on the eve of Saint Valentine's Day 1997, Claude had published a *chronique* commenting on a newly published book, *Le Dico des Mots-caresses* by Marie Treps, about the language of love. Incidentally, it was not until late in the twentieth century that the French adopted the long-established British and American custom of sending commercially produced Valentine cards. In his article Claude takes pleasure in analysing the book, declaring his surprise and astonishment to find such a wealth and variety of terms of endearment.   He quotes not a few of them, interspersed with etymological comments and personal reactions to the examples he selects:

> Ma poule, ma poulette, mon oiseau des îles, mon poussin, ma caille, ma colombe, ma tourterelle *chantent la métaphore de la plume et du duvet—la poule « jeune fille » apparaissant déjà au XIIIe siècle ! L'anthropomorphisme triomphant s'étale dans les fourrures, les pelages :* mon agneau—*et son antagoniste,* mon loup !—ma chatte, mon chaton, mon lapin... Ma biche *aussi—oh les grands yeux tendres, façon Walt Disney !*

Not only does he discover innumerable names of birds and animals used in the language of love but he also encounters examples from the insect world, and writes:

> *Les insectes n'ont de la douceur que dans les mots qui les désignent—leur signifiant vaut mieux que leur signifié !* Ma puce, mon puceron, ma libellule, ma sauterelle *s'imposent par la danse buccale qu'ils mettent en jeu : la « puce » tire les lèvres vers l'avant, dans l'approche d'un petit baiser... Voltaire donnait à Mlle de la Tour du Pin du « mon papillon » !*

He finds to his amazement that there are even names of shell-fish among the hundreds of terms of endearment listed:

> *Les crustacés viennent comme la marée en Carême : Martin du Gard fait saluer une vieille dame par :* « Bonjour, mon vieux crabe ! » *L-F Céline y va du moelleux :* « T'as compris maintenant, ma langouste ? »... *On ne devinerait pas les trésors de tendresse contenus dans un simple :* « Oui, ma crevette ! »

After the crustaceans come inanimate objects, of which Claude writes:

> *Nous autres Français, nous avons eu Rabelais, nous caressons d'atavisme :* « Ha badebec, ma tendrette, ma braguette ! » *disait Pantagruel. Panurge apostrophait Frère Jean d'un « mon bedon », et on se souvient que Sganarelle embrasse passionnément sa bouteille, lui disant: «Ah ma petite friponne ! que je t'aime, mon petit bouchon ! »...*

He then turns to what must be one of the most frequently used terms of endearment: *mon chou.* Giving a history of this expression, he informs his readers that *chou* came into its own with the invention of the famous *chou à la crème* around 1750. This delicious piece of *pâtisserie* soon became a favourite in Paris and Versailles, where the Dauphine addressed her eldest son, the Duke of Burgundy, who died in 1763, *chou d'amour,* a term of endearment familiar to us today. Twenty years later Marie-Antoinette would use the same expression of love when addressing the future Louis XVIII. These terms were in use throughout the nineteenth century and have survived to this day.

The celebrated *chou* is followed by herbs, fruits and vegetables, among which we find *ma belle asperge, mon brin de persil, ma banane, mon artichaut*. Most entertaining of all, however, in Claude's opinion, are the examples in the notices to be found in the press, the special messages intended for one's true love on St Valentine's Day. He quotes two of these from *Libération*:

> *Un homosexuel y appelle quelqu'un* : « Mon petit lapin aux pruneaux », *tandis qu'une femme écrit* : « Mon gros loup au fenouil, je te garde bien au chaud pour longtemps, et encore, et encore… ta morue ».

Claude ends his article with a brief quotation from the closing lines of one of La Fontaine's fables, *Le Lion amoureux*:

> Amour, amour, quand tu nous tiens,
> On peut bien dire : « adieu prudence » !

In the context of *les mots-caresses*, we should take a look at *Ces mots qui changent de sexe au pluriel*, republished on 17 November 2017, where Claude refers to the noun *amour*:

> « Et l'amour, dites-moi ? » *Oh ! l'amour, grande affaire intime ! Pour Vaugelas (1647)* : « Il est masculin et féminin, mais non pas toujours indifféremment, car quand il signifie Cupidon, il ne peut être que masculin, et quand on parle de Dieu ».

Vaugelas states that *l'amour* is masculine, therefore *divin*, not *divine*. He continues, observing that some would say « l'amour des pères et des mères pour leurs enfants est si *pleine* de tendresse », whereas others would insist on « l'amour des pères et des mères pour leurs enfants est si *plein* de tendresse ». *Le vieux Claude* himself prefers the feminine, « selon l'inclination de notre langue qui se porte d'ordinaire au féminin plutôt qu'à l'autre genre », giving as an example: « La petite amour parle, et la grande est muette », to which thought *notre Claude* responds with *: C'est vrai, au fond, comme la douleur…*

Other writers of the seventeenth century suggested that *l'amour* should be masculine in prose and feminine in verse. Duneton is of the opinion that, although such a statement may appear strange, we should remember that poetry was at the time held in rather higher esteem than it is now.

Thomas Corneille, *le petit frère du « Grand »,* gave the rule with which we are all familiar today:

> Quand l'amour est pluriel (…) et qu'il signifie des commerces de passion, il doit être féminin. *Oui, l'amour fou, mais de folles amours.* Les amours enfantines *sont de beaux attachements éprouvés dans l'enfance ;* des amours enfantins *désignerait un sentiment niais, un peu simplet.*

There is often confusion between *le couple* and *la couple.* Claude writes, humorously:

> *Question délicate : faut-il dire* une couple *de pigeons, comme l'affirme votre vieil oncle lettré pendant les repas de famille où on les sert avec des petits pois du jardin ?*

Non is his reply. There is no such rigid rule as your aged uncle would have you believe. *Couple* in that sense ought to be feminine, since it derives from the Latin noun *copula,* but there is no obligation in French to make it so. It was, however, feminine for a long period of time. Du Bellay wrote « Belle couple, heureuse union » and Montaigne « Comme une couple de chevaux attelés ». In the seventeenth century the matter had not yet been decided. Ménage accepted both genders, *un* or *une couple de pigeons.* Claude writes:

> *Il ajoute (c'est essentiel) :* « Comme disent les femmes ». *Cette remarque en dit long : le féminin se sera perpétué en catimini aux cuisines :* « Marguerite nous préparera une couple de pigeons pour le baptême ! » *Cela sent les raffinements de la cuisine bourgeoise de Mme Saint-Ange ; votre vieil oncle a raison !*

However, continues Duneton, one may say *une couple de bœufs, une couple d'heures*—except when *les bœufs* are yoked together, in which case one must say *une paire de bœufs.*

> *Ô nuance !... Pour Richelet (en 1694),* couple *est masculin en parlant des personnes, féminin en parlant d'animaux ou de choses—ce qui paraît d'un systématisme un peu exagéré.*

Another of Duneton's book reviews, first appearing in 2008, concerns the work *Les noms de rues disent la ville* by Jean-Claude Bouvier. The article was reproduced in the electronic version of *Le Figaro* on 1 December 2017 and opens thus:

*S'il y a un pays où la politique se reflète dans la rue, c'est bien la France.
Non seulement le moindre projet de législation précipite les Français sur la
voie publique, mais la ville elle-même leur monte à la tête grâce à une
toponymie hautement politicienne dont on ne doit guère trouver l'équivalent
ailleurs dans le monde. Nous jetons à la voirie le nom des héros !*

This last remark is typical of Claude's well-chosen use of language in order
to create humour, *la voirie* meaning both highway and rubbish dump.

Our *chroniqueur* appreciates the sociological study of street names
provided by this most unusual and surprising book, and he congratulates the
lexicographer, Christine Bonneton, on publishing such a work. *Les Noms de
rues disent la ville* traces the history of street names from the late Middle
Ages, when directions were provided in the most practical manner, for
example at Tournus, where one was called « rue allant de la place de la
petite boucherie à la poterne de l'abbaye » and in Montpellier—and here
Claude cannot resist adding a pertinent aside—where the clear indication
was « traversa que va a las filhas », *passage qui va aux filles, de joie, bien
entendu !*

Street names may recall fountains, trees and wayside crosses as well as
trades and professions. Certain names are derived from signs, especially
those of taverns long since gone, for example « rue du Chapeau-Rouge »,
and others from ovens, mills, and games, such as « rue du Jeu-de-Paume »,
and from institutions of every kind—churches, town-halls and hospitals.

Bouvier's book shows how street names reflect the history of the nation.
The author illustrates how the seventeenth century marks the beginning of
a new era, when names start to arise directly from decisions made by
officialdom rather than springing naturally from popular usage. From that
time onwards we begin to see the commemoration of heroes.

The French Revolution would bring with it a desire to rid the streets of
any trace of Christianity: those bearing saints' names, in Paris and in other
towns and cities, saw those names changed by the simple removal of the
title of sanctity, leaving instead of *la rue Saint-Denis*, *la rue Denis*, and
instead of *la rue Saint-Jacques, la rue Jacques*, and so on. It is not
surprising to learn that some streets were given entirely new names: *les rues
de la Liberté, de la Révolution, de la Constitution,* to name some of those
most frequently found, though there was never, *jamais, bizarrement,*
comments Claude Duneton, *une place de la Guillotine.*

It was in the nineteenth century that political nomenclature gained
prominence, when the names of contemporary heroes were affixed to
buildings on every street corner. Paris, above all, displays the whole
Napoleonic legend, though neither residents nor visitors recognise many of

those once-famous names of generals. Claude wittily writes: *Kellermann ou Rapp, à la rigueur on sait ; Cambronne, on ne connaît que lui !*

Bouvier wishes to point out, however, that some street names can be chronologically misleading: when we see the name J-J Rousseau we have an image of the eighteenth century, whereas we discover that the road in question was not so named until 1905. Similarly, Voltaire's name often appeared after 1870, as a sign of his anti-clericalism more than as a tribute to his literary merits. The *rues du 14-juillet* arrived late, dating from the *triomphe de la République*, between 1880 and 1900. The newly elected municipal authorities used their brooms to sweep clean, making many changes as they played *un grand jeu de chaises musicales*, clearing away any remnants of religion (*donc réactionnaires*) or local history reflected in street names. It was then that streets were renamed Louis Blanc, Raspail, sometimes Robespierre, to bring to mind *une invisible « révolution culturelle »*. It is with amused distaste that Claude concludes his *chronique*:

> *Ce sont les assassinats qui portent bien à la rue ! Jean Jaurès évidemment. Carnot le jeune, Paul Doumer... Et le président Félix Faure ! Sa mort subite, si j'ose dire, est assimilée à un crime. De lèse-phallocrate ?*

It is not only books that Claude reviews. On 15 April 2010, in his article *Un gars qu'a mal tourné*, he writes the critique of a documentary film, *Bernard, ni Dieu ni chaussettes*, made by Pascal Bouche and Bernard Gainier. Not for the first time, nor for the last, does our *chroniqueur* bemoan the fact that so much of cultural value was lost with the gradual disappearance of regional languages and dialects, of which only very few traces have survived.

The documentary, which was produced in Paris, in the *Espace Saint-Michel*, evokes, through the real life of a peasant of Meung-sur-Loire, the poetic work of someone dear to Claude's heart, Gaston Couté, most of whose work, though certainly not all, is written *dans le dialecte des plaines à blé de la Beauce,* says Claude, according to whom Couté is one of the greatest of the French poets of the first decade of the twentieth century:

> *N'en déplaise à personne, il l'est au même titre que Verlaine dont il hanta les erres quelques années après le « pauvre Lélian » dans le Montmartre de la Belle Époque.*

Those years also saw Couté's fellow-poet, Jehan-Rictus, his companion in arms, writing in a very similar genre, that of the speech of the beggar and the outcast, in a quasi duel of despair.

Claude praises the documentary in appropriately poetic terms, writing from the heart:

> *Le plaisir des mots de terroir vieux comme les chemins, doux comme les prunes mûres, forts comme le vin d'avant le phylloxéra, passe par la bouche et par l'oreille dans ce reportage sur le vif à Meung-sur-Loire, où le fleuve s'appelait depuis toujours la Louère...*

With the foresight of a true poet, Gaston Couté, le « gars qu'a mal tourné », cried into the *vent mauvais*—a clear allusion to Verlaine's *Chanson d'automne*—his horror of war, and Claude reminds us—*tenez-vous bien*—that these words were written between 1900 and 1910. He hears in Couté's prophetic words the voices of those peasant conscripts. Although not mentioning the twenty-eight young men of Lagleygeolle, the boys of his *Le Monument*, who went to war, he surely had them in mind as he wrote this *chronique*. Indignant that some critics have undervalued Couté, Claude asserts:

> *Il n'est pas « un obscur poète », il est un rayon de lumière, d'espérance et de tendresse, venu d'un temps où l'homme occidental n'avait pas encore inventé la boucherie humaine.*

Couté died in poverty, of tuberculosis, in the *Hôpital Lariboisière* in Paris, in June 1911. Will there be any marking of the centenary of his death, the tragic extinguishing of this *rayon de soleil*? Claude fears not, yet the centenary of the poet's death was indeed observed in Paris in February 2011 and Couté's renown has continued to increase. This ray of light and hope seems to be illuminating more and more people, as they come to know and appreciate the genius of his poetry: Duneton would be glad.

On 14 October 2010 Claude summarises in *Paroles d'amour* the research carried out by two American academics from the University of Texas, whose study was published in the September 2010 edition of the *Journal of Personality and Social Psychology*. Having taught English for some twenty years, Duneton naturally retains a lively interest in the subject and it is not surprising that he should read research papers on the English language as keenly as he studies those written on the French language. According to Professor James Pennebaker and his co-researcher Molly Ireland, a couple will match each other's style of language more closely during happy times than when the relationship is experiencing difficulties:

> When two people start a conversation, they usually begin talking alike within a matter of seconds […] This also happens when people read a book

or watch a movie. As soon as the credits roll, they find themselves talking like the author or the central characters.

This phenomenon, termed LSM (language style matching), forms the basis of the study under review. Researchers at the University of Texas have been trying to establish whether, and how, romantic love affects one's use of language. Claude is somewhat surprised at this notion and writes: *Il faut être hardi pour avoir des idées pareilles !* Be that as it may; Pennebaker and his colleague have studied the cases of two pairs of poets, one from the nineteenth and the other from the twentieth century. The academics state that those who are deeply in love speak and write in a similar way, in that they each imitate and repeat the vocabulary and sentence structure of the other, but if the relationship grows cold this shared usage collapses and the two seem to become like strangers again. Claude comments:

> *La chose semble naturelle et surprenante à la fois, car il ne s'agit pas simplement d'utiliser les mots de son partenaire en passion, ni des petits mots d'amour que deux êtres en symbiose s'inventent pour leur usage privé—non, c'est toute une syntaxe qui devient similaire, disent les auteurs, avec « les façons d'utiliser les pronoms, les prépositions et d'autres mots dans des phrases diverses ».*

Hundreds of instances have been analysed for this research, and computer programmes have been used to calculate and record the similarities within the linguistic usage of the couples studied. Although Claude is interested in the results of the research, he doubts whether what has been found to be true of the English language would apply equally to French. He is not at all convinced that similar results would emerge, as the characteristics of English and French and their grammatical constructions differ so greatly from each other. He suggests that the frequency of slang words and private expressions used in intimate relationships between French speakers might make a more profitable study, concluding:

> *À mon avis le baromètre du professeur Pennebaker ne sera pas facilement applicable aux French lovers.*

Claude reviews a particularly interesting dictionary on 25 November 2010 in his article *Belgicismes sans frontière*: the *Dictionnaire des belgicismes* by Michel Francard, Geneviève Géron, Régine Wilmet and Aude Wirth. He observes that Belgians have traditionally regarded their brand of French as in some way inferior to the language spoken in France, considering it sullied by the various regional dialects of Wallonia and Picardy and the slang spoken in Brussels. Aware as we are of Claude's championing of regional and minority languages, we are not surprised to find his opinion different from that commonly held: he considers that the French spoken by Belgians is enhanced by those very regional characteristics so often censured. He takes delight in the appearance of this dictionary:

> *C'est là une bonne nouvelle, car notre français commun a besoin de sang neuf ; au plus nous serons de francs parleurs, au plus notre langue ira bien. (Ce* au plus *constitue une délicatesse exposée par le dictionnaire.)*

The Belgians themselves, whom Duneton calls *cette courageuse nation*, have only recently begun to appreciate the beauty of their own local dialects of French, some of which have a very proud history. Instead of hunting down *les belgicismes* in order to condemn them, the new approach, as witnessed by this *Dictionnaire des belgicismes*, is to study, observe, appreciate and describe them.   Claude remarks:

> *Aussi les petites déviances au français dit* « *de référence* » *sont généralement jolies ; elles donnent de la couleur. Quelle importance de dire* « la porte à rue » *ou* « la porte donnant sur la rue » ? « La porte à rue est toujours ouverte. »   *C'est une caresse à l'oreille...*

As a Frenchman interested in minority and regional languages, he admires many of the examples he quotes from the work, one of which is *le frotte-manche*, indicating a servile individual, a flatterer. Of even greater interest to him, however, are the Belgian French words which are used in France, *plus ou moins clandestinement*, and, to his surprise, the terms he himself recognises and remembers from his own upbringing in Corrèze.   The word *chemisette*, for instance, which is defined in this Belgian dictionary as « un sous-vêtement pour les adultes ou les enfants des deux sexes, avec ou sans manches », is immediately familiar to Claude, as his mother, who had never set foot in Belgium, always used it in that sense.   He recalls, too, commenting on the entry *emmanchure*, how his father used the word *emmanche*, to indicate a complicated situation or dubious business, « C'est une drôle d'emmanche », and, from time to time, the full word itself, « C'est une drôle d'emmanchure ». Having searched in vain for the word *emmanchure* in his dictionaries of slang, Claude wonders whether this Belgian expression was an item left over from the language spoken by working men in the period between the two world wars.

The use in Belgium of the expression *plus vite* for *plus tôt* does not surprise him in the least, as this use is also current in France: « Elle sera là demain, elle ne peut pas venir plus vite ».   Claude declares that not only is such usage perfectly normal but it happens to be *une phrase des plus limousines*, whose familiarity obviously delights him.

Soon after that *chronique*, another of Claude's book reviews appears: *On pouffe, mais en lettré*, on 13 January 2011, and was one of several articles he had written in advance, *pour le cas où...* In this *chronique* he admits he would never normally have thought of picking up a book with such a title as *Petit Abécédaire du rire* but because he had read on the cover that the preface was by Paul Fournel, *président de l'Oulipo* (Ouvroir de Littérature Potentielle), a man of discernment, an enchanting writer and *un humoriste talentueux*, he bought a copy. Such a foreword, says Claude, guarantees that the book in question is worth reading and will not turn out to be *de la gnognote*. He writes:

> *J'ai ouvert le livre, et j'ai ri. Mais attention, il ne s'agit pas chez Monsieur Meunier du gros rire Ah Ah Ah Ah ! des andouillettes ! On pouffe, mais en lettré—et toutes les allusions savantes ne sont pas immédiatement déchiffrables dans un livre qui cite Arthur Cravan, André Frédérique, Alphonse Allais et 162 autres—je les ai comptés.*

This *Petit Abécédaire du rire et de ses environs* by Claude Meunier is indeed very amusing, but our *chroniqueur* comments further:

> *C'est un livre de dérapages sémantiques, de rires en coin, de simples ricanements avec quelques éclats épars...*

Duneton elaborates on the kind of humour offered by Meunier, some of it based on gentle childhood memories and comical family situations, while other parts reveal a background of vulgar talk, dirty jokes, suggestive language, crude stories—all dependent on word-play. Sometimes the humour is subtle and not at all obvious, whereas on occasion it is blatantly silly. Claude quotes one or two instances of clever manipulation of language, among which is the following, which I, in common with many reading this book, have encountered more than once before:

> Six Russes, c'est six Slaves, si s'lave c'est qu'y s'nettoie, si ce n'est toi c'est donc ton frère.

As well as the puns and jokes, there are pages of fine writing. Having remarked that Meunier interlards his text with wise reflections on life and art and having remarked on his easy, natural style, Claude quotes from Paul Fournel's *préface*:

On se demande en fin de compte […] si Meunier n'aime pas tout simplement
la langue et les hommes qui l'écrivent et la lisent.

To this comment Claude adds: *« Je le crois—les femmes aussi »* and closes
his *chronique* with an enchanting schoolboy howler:

En tout cas il serait très bon en candidat au bac de nos jours où l'on trouve
dans des copies de sciences naturelles : « Un ver solitaire est un ver qui vit
tout seul à la campagne ».

As we have seen so far in this chapter, the *chroniques* of Claude Duneton
in *Le Figaro littéraire*, like those of Aristide before him, often take the form
of book and film reviews.   A further instance of this feature is his critique
of *Les godillots sont lourds*, a work by Maurice Fombeure, first published
in 1948, a book he has chosen to reread and review as he wishes to compare
the French language of the 1930s and 1940s, especially *le langage familier*,
with that of today. He writes:

Le langage familier des années 1930-1940 a pris une teinte démodée aussi
pleine de nostalgie qu'une écriture à l'encre violette sur une feuille fanée...
Personne ne dit plus spontanément : « Ça me botte ! » *pour dire «* Ça me
plaît, ça me convient *», sauf peut-être par ironie.*

Citing other examples, Claude expresses his particular enjoyment of this
book, probably because Maurice Fombeure is a poet who has recorded in
elegant prose his accounts of « la drôle de guerre », from signing up in
September 1939 to his demobilisation in July 1940. As he writes his
mémoires, he describes incidentally the utter chaos and incompetence of an
army so completely unprepared for the German onslaught.
    Fombeure uses familiar French, though never resorting to slang, as befits
a man of forty-two, someone of refinement, a former schoolmaster and
published poet, whose work, Claude emphasises, had already appeared in
the *Nouvelle Revue Française*.   In 1948, then, *le sergent* Fombeure uses
expressions which are frankly already old-fashioned, such as « il y a du pied
dans la chaussette » (*il y a du bon, de l'espoir, de quoi se réjouir*), an absurd
image, typical of the expressions used by soldiers serving in the First World
War but still in common use as late as 1950.   Although such examples are
of interest to Claude, he prefers to examine items which, though dated, are
still in current use, of the type: *« Dis donc, vieux »,* a mode of address
regularly used among pals.
    Claude says of the adjective *épatant*, which remains in use and is still
understood, that it had its heyday in the period 1920-1930 and has now
acquired *comme une odeur de bouchon, si l'on voit ce que je veux dire,*

having been superseded by the omnipresent *super*. He quotes Maurice Fombeure, adding his own comment: « J'ai entendu dire que vous avez à votre bureau un type épatant », *écrit Fombeure—c'est gentiment désuet.*

The verb *blaguer* has lost its former frequency, too: « Tu blagues ? » for « Tu veux rire ? » is now more likely to be heard in old people's homes, says Claude, as it has been replaced in the speech of young people with the vulgar « Tu déconnes ? ». *Hélas !* Claude sighs, and goes on to quote the hypothetical report of a fictitious senior officer on his imaginary sergeant: « A tendance à blaguer avec les camarades », which would be expressed differently today: « A tendance à plaisanter ». Claude remarks that although the use of the verb has declined, the corresponding noun is still very much alive:

> « C'est de la blague, c'est une blague » *ont gardé de la fraîcheur—surtout la locution* « sans blague », *qui veut dire* « c'est vrai », ou « sincèrement ». *Seul le verbe s'est assoupi.*

The English word "because" (*Dieu sait que nous ne sommes pas privés de mots anglais !* remarks Claude), was once very fashionable, especially in the period 1925-1955. Fombeure uses it incorrectly, as Claude points out, although one might perhaps applaud Fombeure for being syntactically more aware here than our *chroniqueur* and indeed than those others who use "because" to translate *à cause de* rather than *parce que*. The example censured by Claude is: « une gaucherie assez désinvolte *because de* ses grands membres ». Fombeure inserts *de* as he obviously knows that "because of" (*à cause de*) would be required here in English, the conjunction "because" on its own being the equivalent of *parce que* and not *à cause de*. Writing of Fombeure's erroneous use of "because" in French, Claude adds:

> *C'était en fait un mot légèrement gourmet, qui sentait son collège, volontiers dans la bouche de professeurs ou de fonctionnaires :* « Il n'est pas venu *because* la grève des transports ».

Although *because* was certainly used in French with the meaning *à cause de*—and one still encounters it occasionally—it may surprise us that Claude, who has such a good command of English, should judge Fombeure's logical, though strictly speaking incorrect, addition of *de*, so harshly and unsympathetically.

Claude is a keen observer of *les glissements de sens* and finds several instances in Fombeure's book. One example he quotes is the expression *couper la chique à quelqu'un*, in the sense of interrupting someone in mid-sentence, *lui couper la parole,* a use which seems to be losing ground:

> J'essayais de justifier mon éclipse partielle.   Il me coupa la chique : Ça suffit !

Today *couper la chique* (which takes us back to the era of pipe-smoking) is normally used to convey the degree of astonishment that renders one speechless:

> *J'ai vu la moto gicler à trois mètres en l'air avant de s'écraser sur l'autoroute : ça m'a coupé la chique.*

Fombeure uses a very rare word, a short-lived familiar term for *kilomètre: kilosto.* The example quoted is:

> Il faut y monter par une route en lacets pendant plus d'un kilosto.

Claude does not think he has heard this word since the end of the 1940s,

> *lorsque mon* « tonton Roger », *un Parigot cycliste qui avait fait le Vél'd'Hiv' avant 39, se vantait au retour d'une randonnée :* « Cinquante *kilostos* dans les jantes ! » *Le* « kilosto » *vaut bien une madeleine, sans doute.*

Our *chroniqueur* is always passionately interested in the history of words. A peculiarity of the French language—*une bizarrerie*—and in this instance also of the English language, since we use the same term, is the use of *matinée* for an afternoon performance.   On 25 March 2010 in *La matinée des autres* Claude devotes almost the whole of his article to this anomaly:

> *La logique de la langue prime parfois sur la logique du sens. Voyez par exemple cette histoire de pièces de théâtre qui sont données en matinée alors qu'elles sont jouées l'après-midi ; les coutumes ont eu beau faire changer l'heure des spectacles, l'expression est restée figée sur la logique des mots alors que le sens devenait absurde.*

He illustrates this point by explaining how, under the *Ancien Régime*, the first meal of the day, in keeping with sound etymology, was called *le déjeuner*, though it is odd that the word so readily lost the circumflex of *jeûne*. The second meal, which was eaten around one o'clock, was called *le dîner*, sharing the same etymology, both words alluding to the breaking of one's fast—*la rupture du jeûne*—first *au déjeuner* and then *au dîner*. A theatrical performance taking place before *le dîner* was therefore held *en matinée,* starting around half-past ten in the morning. This performance was logically so called to distinguish it from *la période vespérale* during which the evening performance took place. We may wonder what happened. Claude explains that during the *Révolution très franco-parisienne* of 1789 meal times began to move little by little towards the evening. Some say that the reason was the shortage of food in Paris, where the ordinary people went hungry, while the revolutionary *élite* lunched around noon « à la fourchette », that is, sumptuously:

> *Dans le même mouvement, le dîner glissait graduellement vers le soir : il passa à 3 heures, puis 5 heures de l'après-midi, pour atteindre au cours du XIXe siècle les 7 et 8 heures du soir. Mais on continua à donner des spectacles « avant le dîner »—et l'on continua à dire qu'ils avaient lieu en matinée, alors que la matinée de l'horloge était passée depuis belle lurette ! Tel le voulut la logique imperturbable des mots.*

Claude is at pains to inform us that this change in meal-times applied at first only to Paris. Elsewhere people continued to time their meals as before, enjoying a good, filling *déjeuner* in the morning and a hearty *dîner* at noon. This situation lasted until the arrival of the television, *le début de « l'ère téléïenne »,* which brought the rest of France into line with Paris, although it probably took a little longer for the people of Montpellier or Esquelbecq to catch up, adds Claude.

> *« Nous avons fait un bon dîner » faisait allusion à un gueuleton de la mi-journée, ce qui ne simplifiait pas la communication dans le domaine du coup de fourchette. Si vous étiez invités « à dîner » par une famille de Brive-la-Gaillarde il fallait vous faire habilement préciser si on vous espérait à midi ou le soir. L'incertitude était totale : cela dépendait de l'âge des amphitryons, de leur degré de modernisme, s'ils étaient souvent allés à Paris ou non...*

Today it is rather easier, as the television has succeeded in unifying French meal times—and much else besides. The only *bizarrerie* is that on both sides of *la Manche* we continue to go to the theatre in the afternoon to see a *matinée* performance!

CHAPTER EIGHT

LE LANGAGE FÉMINISTE AND *L'ÉCRITURE INCLUSIVE*

> *Les langues qui possèdent un genre neutre sont favorisées à ce jeu-là ; le monde anglo-saxon, où le* politically correct *tourne à l'obsession, place tous ses efforts dans l'effacement grammatical des genres [...]*
> —Claude Duneton, *L'amour du neutre,* 26 February 1998, *Le Figaro*

The questions surrounding feminist language and the equality of the sexes present many problems, one of which is succinctly expressed by Grevisse in his *Le Bon Usage* (1980: §423):

> Le féminisme, ayant conquis l'accès à toutes les dignités ou fonctions jusque-là réservées à des hommes, se plaît à conquérir aussi l'usage des appellations masculines correspondant à ces dignités ou fonctions (même dans le cas où la langue possède une forme féminine).

Some of the linguistic problems in this domain predate the feminist movement. In our dictionaries we find several feminine forms of nouns denoting professions, where there is a certain lack of clarity, since some of those feminine forms serve two distinct functions. When we look up the noun *le cuisinier* we find its feminine form, *la cuisinière*, but this word can mean either a female cook or an item of kitchen equipment—an electric or gas cooker. It has a third meaning, though admittedly rather rare in modern French society: *la femme du cuisinier*! This kind of confusion applies to many nouns, where it is only from the context that one can determine the meaning.

In today's society we find that most women who are carrying out the work formerly done by men prefer to be called by the masculine term despite the existence of a well-established feminine equivalent. Where the title of a profession ends in *e* the problem does not arise, since women are pleased to be *la maire, la ministre* or *la juge*. When the masculine noun ends in *-eur* there is a baffling choice to be made: is *le professeur* to become *la professeure*? Is *le chroniqueur* to become *la chroniqueure*? There is here no discernible pattern. Alice Develey of *Le Figaro littéraire* styles herself *chroniqueuse*, yet this seems to go against the normal rules of French, which would expect such a feminine form to be based on a masculine noun ending in *-eux*. Duneton mentions this precise point in his *chronique* dated 11 November 1999, *Le féminin compliqué*, to which we referred in Chapter Four. There is obviously considerable *flottement* in this matter.

It has been interesting to observe the ease with which Parisians have become accustomed to refer to *la Maire de Paris*, Anne Hidalgo, humorously called by some « la reine-maire ». There has never been any question of calling her *mairesse*, a feminine form which she would have found demeaning, as it can denote the wife of a mayor. The question of status is all-important to those women who have achieved equality with men in positions and professions which have traditionally been the preserve of males. Their unwillingness to accept a title such as *mairesse* or *poétesse* is perhaps understandable. Indeed very many women are of this persuasion and such is equally the case in Britain, where a woman in the acting profession often insists on being called *actor*, shunning not a modern feminised term but the traditional feminine form, *actress*, in constant use since 1700. The complexities of feminist language are legion.

In his article *L'amour du neutre* of 26 February 1998 (which appeared in the online edition of *Le Figaro* on 1 September 2017, under the heading *Pourquoi la langue sexuée pose-t-elle un problème ?)* Claude Duneton takes up the perennial theme of linguistic equality between men and women. As we are aware, this concern has been evident in French government and society for several decades, becoming a matter of urgency in the 1980s and even more pressing by the second decade of the twenty-first century.

Duneton traces the history of the two grammatical genders in French, acknowledging the serious difficulties encountered when writers and speakers attempt to adapt the language to modern life, where people at every level engage in intense grammatical discussion concerning such matters as the feminine forms of professional titles. After the many years of debate, involving all Francophone countries, matters have still not been settled to everyone's satisfaction. No doubt *l'usage* will eventually establish a new norm.

Such considerations reflect the unease in society surrounding the dignity of the human person. Our *chroniqueur* regards the ongoing discussions as being outside the usual spheres of traditionalism and modernism and says of *le débat*:

> *Il met en lumière le besoin impérieux de neutralité qui se fait jour dans le monde contemporain, et d'un autre côté la nature profondément sexuée de la langue française.*

He explains how the structure of modern French is inherited from Vulgar Latin, which was inevitably influenced by the various indigenous languages. Whereas classical Latin had a neuter gender as well as the masculine and feminine, this was gradually lost, almost all neuter nouns becoming masculine in French. Thus Old French emerged with only two genders. Although Claude regrets, from some points of view, that inanimate objects have a gender in French, quoting as examples *la route* and *le chemin*—*la route* being feminine because it derives from *via rupta*, an open road *cut through* a forest, reduced to *rupta* and obviously feminine, *le chemin* being masculine because of its Celtic root *cam*, which evolved into the masculine *camino*—in fact he values the convenient distinction in meaning and usage between these two words of different genders, a characteristic to be found throughout the French language:

> *Il est vrai que le masculin possède un degré d'abstraction, de généralisation : on quitte* le droit chemin, le chemin du ciel est semé d'épines, *etc., tandis qu'on prend, matériellement,* la route, on fait bonne route, *ou concrètement aussi* fausse route.

Claude concedes that this single example does not provide any sure basis on which to work, though he maintains that feminine nouns tend to find themselves imbued with certain values and qualities, for instance gentleness and beauty, whereas masculine nouns, despite arguments to the contrary, convey a certain notion of strength and virility:

> *Cela est clair dans les doublets, du type* le grain—*celui que l'on broie, que l'on achète*—et *la* graine chargée de fécondité. La table *est accueillante, maternelle, surtout quand elle est « mise », alors que* le bureau *est austère, en quelque sorte sévèrement paternel. Nous n'y pouvons rien ; la représentation du réel se colore en français, à notre insu, de teintes insolites qui contribuent à notre originalité et probablement au charme de la langue...*

He considers that it is this very feature that creates a certain internal tension today, when the western world aspires to remove the differences between men and women, male and female, masculine and feminine. The egalitarian ideal would be for any function to have a genderless name.

Languages able to express gender neutrality have a distinct advantage in this context. The English-speaking world, where political correctness is almost an obsession, goes to great lengths to rid the language of any hint of gender:

Le monde anglo-saxon [...] place tous ses efforts dans l'effacement grammatical des genres, au prix d'acrobaties syntaxiques qui défient parfois le bon sens. Dans un imprimé d'enquête avant embauche, où le « demandeur » d'emploi est nommé applicant *(neutre, ou épicène), l'une des questions est rédigée ainsi :* Did the applicant leave your employ of *their* own accord? *(La personne postulante a-t-elle quitté l'emploi de* leur *propre chef ?)*

Those of us who love the English language and care about grammar and logic regret such linguistic developments—grammatical absurdities—and are saddened to see their increasing presence and their gradual acceptance as the norm. Even the Church of England, in order to please certain influential members of the General Synod, has decided to remove any suggestion that God might be male by changing the pivotal congregational response at the heart of the Eucharist, "It is right to give Him thanks and praise" to "It is right to give thanks and praise", a logically and grammatically—and some would say theologically—unsatisfactory solution, and a quite pointless exercise, since elsewhere in the liturgy God is regarded and addressed as Father...

One reads and hears such ungrammatical statements in English as the following, even when the subject is unequivocally feminine and singular, "Each girl was required to give *their* name", or clearly masculine and singular, as in "Anthony's education is stated on *their* CV". In the face of such examples, where there is no ambiguity, one cannot help wondering whether the use of "their" will eventually become accepted by grammarians, as has long since been the case with the singular pronouns "everyone", "someone" and "no one", which are invariably found with the plural possessive "their", as no acceptable alternative exists in the modern language. It is the intention which has changed: the avoidance of using *his* and *her*.

Un pluriel aberrant alors qu'il s'agit d'une seule personne, afin d'éviter d'écrire his *ou* her. *L'amour du neutre conduit nos voisins à tordre le cou à leur grammaire ! La violence du procédé nous étonne : la grammaire française est trop fondée sur la logique pour pouvoir se livrer à de telles hérésies...*

So wrote Duneton at the time, never imagining what would happen within the space of two decades. On 5 October 2017, on the front page of *Le Figaro,* there appeared the *Éditorial* by Étienne de Montety, under the heading « Pauvres lecteur·rice·s ! ». It opened:

Elle s'insinue dans les textes officiels. Le Haut Comité [*recte* Conseil] à l'égalité la préconise dans un manuel à l'adresse des « acteur·rice·s de la communication institutionnelle, et des lecteur·rice·s curieux et curieuses de la démarche de communication égalitaire ». De quoi s'agit-il ? De l'écriture inclusive...

Although we cannot know for certain how Claude Duneton would have reacted to this typographically extraordinary solution to the problem of gender inequality in language, we are mindful of his cautious approach to spelling reform and his reluctance to accept any change in the written word which might obscure etymology. At the same time, however, he would probably have admired the principle of fairness behind *l'écriture inclusive*, having admitted both *le besoin impérieux de neutralité qui se fait jour dans le monde contemporain* and *la nature profondément sexuée* of the French language; not that this new style of writing results in any kind of neutrality, since all it does is to show masculine and feminine forms side by side and of equal value. Claude would certainly have rejected the awkward orthographic and typographic requirements of the new system. The difficulties involved in producing *l'écriture inclusive* would have shocked him as much as the grammatical gymnastics he had witnessed in those politically correct—though logically and linguistically reprehensible—samples of English we saw earlier.

It was, however, almost as if he had foreseen some kind of strange development when writing his *L'amour du neutre* twenty years ago:

Mais cela donne une idée de l'âpreté de l'effort à fournir chez nous où, nous laissant guider par le penchant millénaire de la langue, il est question au contraire de mettre au pas les ils *et les* elles, *les* le *et les* la. *La joute ne fait que commencer !*

How right he was! The jousting did not begin in earnest until July 2013, when *Le Haut Conseil à l'égalité entre les femmes et les hommes* published a press statement, summarising its findings and recommendations. Further communiqués and papers would appear over the next three years, culminating in the publication by Mots-Clés in September 2017 of the *Manuel d'écriture inclusive*, a twenty-page booklet recommended by the *Haut Conseil* itself.

We cannot imagine what Claude would have said about the use of the mid-point in order to include the feminine visibly in this clumsy attempt at producing gender equality in writing. We can, however, be fairly certain that he would not have accepted a type of spelling which renders reading aloud an impossibility, unless one is prepared to read everything out in full. Thus Étienne de Montety's way of addressing his readers would have to be

« pauvres lecteurs et lectrices », which would sound artificial and repetitious and would impair the fluency of the spoken language: one such instance is perhaps acceptable but when it is necessary to treat all such cases similarly, not only nouns but often adjectives too, it becomes ponderous and tedious.

The reaction from some feminists is positive and supportive, as one might expect, though some are very strongly opposed to such a system. There have been several articles in the press, including *Le Figaro*, many of them dated October 2017 and most of them highly critical of *l'écriture inclusive*. The *Académie française* sees in this system « un peril mortel » for the future of the French language.

Antoine Gautier, a lecturer in French Language at the University of Paris-Sorbonne and a researcher in French syntax and linguistics, explains that the main argument in favour of such a fundamental change is that people, women in particular, object to the assumption in modern French that the masculine must always take precedence, a notion unpalatable to many feminists. Schoolchildren are taught that « le masculin l'emporte sur le féminin » in all cases of agreement—and girls do not like it.

In older French, that is, prior to the seventeenth century, agreements tended to be made according to the position within the phrase or clause of the element requiring an agreement, for example, « Les hommes et les femmes sont belles ». Since the adjective here is nearer to *femmes* it becomes feminine plural. To introduce that type of agreement now, as a few teachers have already done this academic year (2017-2018), would create a grammar visibly so different from the traditional version that it would cause untold confusion, and, if coupled with *l'écriture inclusive,* would complicate the teaching and learning of the French language to such an extent that the process would become intolerably chaotic.

Much has been written about feminist and inclusive language over the past fifty years and many possible solutions to the problems have been aired by official bodies, including *l'Académie française*. Those grammarians and linguists who have studied the subject in depth are often perplexed by the attitude adopted by some feminists, who, as we have seen, reject the feminised professional titles proposed, as they do not like to be called *écrivaine*, *poétesse* or *avocate,* finding these forms condescending and demeaning; their argument is that they object to being identified first as women before being defined as people. The other objection is that a separate feminine form devalues the character of the professional title. Solomon himself would have difficulty in establishing precisely *ce que femme veut*.

CONCLUSION

L'HÉRITAGE OF CLAUDE DUNETON

La langue française n'est pas véritablement la langue des Français.
—Claude Duneton, *La mort du français,* Plon, 1999, page 27.

Claude Duneton has left behind him a generous legacy of fine writing—
novels; books on language and education, containing much material of an
autobiographical nature; reference works and dictionaries of *expressions
imagées* and, not least, the entertaining and informative *chroniques* he wrote
for *Le Figaro littéraire*, erudite columns, full of passion. The subject
matter of his *chroniques du langage* could be said to reflect every facet of
his wider literary work: the history of words and phrases and their precise
meaning; his love of word-play and colourful metaphor; his sarcastic wit
and subtle use of irony; his regret at the disappearance of regional
languages, especially *l'occitan*, and their replacement with *la langue
française*, which is in fact the language of Paris and the Île de France.
    One might wonder sometimes whether there is in Claude Duneton's
opinions, as expressed in his *chroniques du langage* and elsewhere, a certain
inconsistency: on the one hand he declares himself firmly against the state
imposition on the nation of a standard French language, regarding it not only
as an impediment to the natural evolution of the language but also as the
principal factor in the virtual obliteration of minority languages and their
cultures; yet on the other hand he has striven to defend that very same
standard language, *le français central*, and has fought for its survival,
joining, and even writing for, the Association *La Défense de la langue
française*, all the while maintaining that the language had suffered from
being regulated. He sometimes contrasts the development of French with
that of English and other languages, which, in his opinion, have been
allowed to evolve freely, without any official interference.
    Duneton treasures the language of La Fontaine and of earlier writers—
Rabelais, Du Bellay and Ronsard—unspoilt by the restrictions so beloved
of Malherbe and his followers. In his *chroniques du langage* Duneton traces
the history of the language he loves through its literature, from the twelfth
century onwards, through its classical, romantic and modern periods, always

defending its evolution and disapproving of the impact on its development of such negative influences as that of the celebrated Malherbe, who, as we have noted, had held a very narrow view of poetry and, when aided and abetted by his admirers, had been instrumental in stunting the natural growth of the language.

Although, as we have seen, Claude defends the correct use of the standard modern language, nothing pleases him more than the acknowledgment and reinstatement by the *Académie française* of regional items of vocabulary, *les belgicismes* and words and expressions from his native *occitan*. If the French language is to survive the continued threat of Anglo-Americanism, it must be ready to welcome non-standard forms and adopt words and expressions from the rest of the French-speaking world. Claude supports wholeheartedly the inclusion of Belgian and Canadian forms, especially as so many of them can be traced back to the traditional French language of old.

Our *chroniqueur* is always delighted to recognise in non-Hexagonal French a word or expression known to him personally from his *corrézien* background and he wishes fervently to embrace *la Francophonie* in all its rich variety in order to empower and promote the French language in the world. He is aware of an unfortunate tendency among some of his compatriots to overlook the importance of French language and culture abroad. Rather than bemoaning the parlous state of the modern language, riddled as it is with Anglo-American vocabulary and syntax, Duneton wishes his readers to remember and appreciate the universal influence of French language and culture throughout the centuries.

Despite the apparent pessimism of its title, Claude's book, *La Mort du français*, published by Plon in 1999, in fact offered a ray of hope. As Pierre Monette of the Plon publishing house commented, Duneton had concluded that the moribund language would not be helped by the continued negative attitude of « Dites…, ne dites pas… » but by being open to all the possible ways of speaking French, although this would of necessity entail risks. Claude had likened the French tongue to a tender pot plant: it would now be necessary to transplant this delicate seedling into the rich soil of popular language, which had been treated for far too long by officialdom as a bed of weeds. Monette ends his review thus:

> Avec *La Mort du français*, Claude Duneton nous invite à arrêter de pleurer les préciosités perdues du subjonctif, et à nous rendre compte que la beauté du français n'est pas dans le ronron des alexandrins de Racine, mais dans la verve d'un Rabelais.

Politically Claude was openly on the left and proud of being a *soixante-huitard*—a rebel, a dissident and a nonconformist! Yet, was he? At times he seemed, in later life, to have joined the ranks of the conventional *bourgeoisie*, not only writing for *Le Figaro* but also contributing articles to *La Défense de la langue française*, although at all times remaining a champion of the language of the people, gently mocking Voltaire for his undoubted snobbery, as we saw in Chapter Four.

Claude was a thoroughly good man: he believed in God; he was a moralist; he had high standards—though perhaps not of the superficial kind, as he did not always dress in the way some of his friends would have liked!—and would have gladly returned to that golden age when *le maître d'école* had dictated to his pupils, so musically, those long, grammatically exacting passages, specially selected from the finest literature. By hearing such extracts children had learned to understand and appreciate the French language and thus to write it correctly

Duneton had a somewhat eccentric view of *l'usage*. It would surely have surprised him to see, almost two decades later, the reappearance and continued metaphorical use of the word *sauvageon*, which, in his idiosyncratic terminology, was an example of *le bel usage* and therefore not expected to endure. In common with other newspapers and the media in general, *Le Figaro* reported on 10 October 2016 that police officers had been attacked by youths—*sauvageons*—who had been throwing Molotov cocktails. Since the first recorded use in December 1999 of the term *sauvageons*, in the sense of young miscreants, by Jean-Pierre Chevènement, then *ministre de l'Intérieur*, the word has been used by other politicians in similar contexts. Bernard Cazeneuve, another *ministre de l'Intérieur*, who would later become *Premier ministre*, used the word and was censured for his *maladresse* by Manuel Valls, *Premier ministre* at the time:

> Le premier ministre a dénoncé l'excès de « mises en cause » dont les policiers et gendarmes font l'objet, tentant de faire oublier la maladresse du ministre de l'Intérieur, qui avait qualifié de simples « sauvageons » les lanceurs de cocktails Molotov à la Grande Borne.

Linguists and grammarians, as well as ordinary readers of his many literary works, will long remember Claude Duneton for his writing. Five years after his death, our *chroniqueur* was being remembered and celebrated in his native Corrèze. In November 2017, there was a *Forum Claude Duneton* at the *Foire du livre de Brive*, and at Beynat a new covered market was opened, bearing his name. These facts were recorded on 10 November, when *Le Figaro* printed his photograph, under the heading *Claude Duneton, ce Monument,* followed by a long report, a part of which now follows:

Alors que s'ouvre ce week-end la Foire du livre de Brive, le village de Beynat, en Corrèze, baptise sa halle du nom de l'écrivain. Sa chevelure blanche tutoyant ses épaules, ce regard cobalt qui vous traverse et ce rire voilé, un peu sourd, qui secoue un corps trapu.

Le Figaro mistakenly names his weekly article *Au plaisir des mots,* which, as we are aware, is the name of the collection of his articles.   This error seems to have become firmly fixed at *Le Figaro* as elsewhere:

Voilà l'image que l'on garde de Claude Duneton, écrivain, traducteur de Shakespeare, philologue, comédien, acteur, chanteur et ancien du Figaro littéraire (il y tenait une délicieuse chronique, « Au plaisir des mots »), disparu en mars 2012.

Brive (Brive-la-Gaillarde), where Claude had been apprenticed as a boy, is a town some thirty kilometres from Lagleygeolle; the village of Beynat is barely ten kilometres away. The reference to *ce Monument* reflects the deserved fame won for him by his *roman vrai,* his factual novel, *Le Monument,* which appeared in 2005. His elder daughter, Louise, had helped him significantly in his research for the book, accompanying him on his investigative journeys.

LE MONUMENT

The war memorial at Lagleygeolle had remained in Claude's memory from his childhood, when during a remembrance ceremony his father had shouted out, to the deep embarrassment of all present: « Ah nom de Dieu, elle était belle la guerre ! Vous pouvez en faire des simagrées. Ça vous va bien ! » A few days before his death, his father would again cry out, pleading this time: « Pourquoi ils ne m'ont pas tué à Verdun ? » It was almost as though Claude had written the book on behalf of his father, from whom he had heard so many gruelling accounts of the 1914-18 war. No one from Lagleygeolle had actually died at Verdun: they had all died at the Somme. Many critics consider *Le Monument* to be Duneton's greatest work, and it is certain that the memorial and the names of the fallen engraved on it have been immortalised by that book.

To the end Claude loved the land of his birth, Corrèze, and above all his home village of Lagleygeolle and his grandparents' house at Antignac, where he spent much of his time in later years. In a rather more substantial obituary of Claude, written by his friend Jean Meyssignac and published in *France-Catholique*, the leading French Catholic weekly, on Wednesday 28 March 2012, exactly one week after Duneton's death, we read intimate details unknown to other journalists. Meyssignac had known Claude and his family all his life and shared their background. Not only did I find this illuminating obituary on the website of *France-Catholique* but I also read a personal tribute submitted by an Italian woman who had lived *au pair* with the Dunetons, Sabrina Nenni, now teaching French in Italy; she had known Claude and his second wife, Isabelle, and had looked after their two daughters for a year.

Meyssignac had witnessed the genuine pain and grief expressed by those who had known Duneton on learning of his death. They had been visibly moved and had shown true sorrow at his loss. Many articles had been written in tribute to him, and some, those appearing in *La Croix* and *Le Figaro*, for example, had demonstrated an unusual warmth. Duneton was hailed as a learned man, an accomplished novelist, a well-known actor and an acknowledged authority on educational matters; he was regarded by some as possibly the greatest writer of his generation.   It was not, however, his accomplishments that were the reason for people's intense sadness, but:

> Notre Duneton était aimable, accueillant, affable, disponible, il était bon d'une bonté de bon aloi, directe, simple, sans manière ; il était bon comme le bon pain. Il ne se prenait pas pour Duneton-du-Figaro-Littéraire. Dès le premier contact c'était évident. Avec ses cheveux en bataille, sa barbe de quelques jours, ses yeux bleus et son sourire gentiment moqueur (« mouquandier » en patois limousin), sa bonté éclatait. Notre Claude était beau. Plus le temps passait plus il était beau.

The true reason for the deep sorrow experienced by those who had known Claude was simply that he was loved—and hence sincerely mourned. He was indeed a beautiful person, a delightful human being, dearly loved by all who knew him.

His difficult childhood, described in the Introduction, was made all the harder for him by his hip dysplasia, which would affect him adversely for the rest of his life. Jean Meyssignac, whose parents had been the proprietors of the local *auberge* at Meyssac, where all the Lagleygeolle *commune* would congregate and exchange news, tells us that Claude, always accompanied by his mother, went to Paris for surgical treatment, not once but several times over the years. Noémie, too, tells me the same. Although Duneton had a limp and would always have some difficulty walking, and would for many years experience pain, he was at least enabled to lead an otherwise normal life, thanks to the operations he had undergone during childhood and later.

As Meyssignac came from Meyssac, he was familiar with Lagleygeolle and all the people and places known to Claude. From him we gain several supplementary items of information—that his parents' *auberge* features in *Le Monument*, for instance, and that Claude lived in Antignac in his grandparents' house, rather than in Lagleygeolle, when he was not in Paris. Jean recalls intimate details of Claude's early life:

> De la fin de sa scolarité primaire à la reprise de ses études vers quinze ans, Duneton vécut une période particulièrement noire et angoissante. Comment avec de mauvaises jambes envisager la vie très dure d'un paysan ? Il m'a confié un jour qu'il pleurait en ramassant l'herbe pour les lapins. C'est là que son courage s'enracine.

He tells us that Claude felt happy and truly at home in the hamlet of Antignac, surrounded by friends and neighbours « chez qui il allait manger la soupe ». Apart from installing water and an electricity supply, he had kept his grandparents' house intact, and he still cooked on the open hearth with traditional equipment—*la crémaillère et le trépied*. Claude was the only person Meyssignac knew who had continued to use an ancient, now obsolete, utensil for hand-washing:

> un petit récipient en zinc prolongé par un tube de plus en plus effilé. Avait-il un nom en français ? En patois, on l'appelait : « la couade ».

Jean reports that the day after his death in Lille Claude was taken back to that old house in Antignac, where his four children came to keep a two-day vigil over his body.

The two friends had often discussed religion. We have seen from his writing that Duneton had a religious faith. Jean tells us that Claude used to attend mass at Meyssac on high days and holy days. When a priest had been accused of paedophilia, in strange circumstances, Claude had defended him, sending « une lettre courageuse et belle » to the court.

We saw earlier, in Chapter One, Claude's reluctance to criticise or censure others, though he does defend himself occasionally, as for example:

> *Certes, je suis loin d'être infaillible, et pas plus qu'un autre à l'abri d'une grosse bévue ; mais pour cette fois au moins ce sont mes censeurs…*

and sometimes becomes bold when despairing of people's obduracy:

> *Les gens préfèrent le mensonge plutôt que d'avoir à réviser leur opinion.*

As if to show his friend's innate modesty and essential lack of self-confidence, Jean Meyssignac ends his obituary by quoting what Claude had confided in a personal letter to him, after appearing in a rather difficult *Apostrophes* programme on Antenne 2 with Bernard Pivot:

> *J'ai été mauvais. Ce n'est pas un métier d'être le marchand de soi-même.*

Perhaps the greatest accolade that Claude could receive in death is the weekly reproduction of his *chroniques du langage* in the digital edition of *Le Figaro*, where he continues to be held in the highest regard both by his *confrères* and by his *fidèles lecteurs*:

> Retrouvez les chroniques de Claude Duneton (1935-2012) chaque semaine. Écrivain, comédien et grand défenseur de la langue française, il tenait avec gourmandise la rubrique *Le plaisir des mots* dans les pages du *Figaro littéraire*.

SELECT BIBLIOGRAPHY: CLAUDE DUNETON

Parler croquant, Stock, 1973
Je suis comme une truie qui doute, Seuil, 1976
Anti-manuel de français, with J-P Gagliano, Seuil, 1978
Le Diable sans porte, Seuil, 1981
La Goguette et la Gloire, Le Pré-aux-Clercs, 1984
À hurler le soir au fond des collèges, with F Pages, Seuil, 1984
Le Chevalier à la charrette, with M. Baile, Albin Michel, 1985
Petit Louis dit XIV, Seuil, 1985
L'Ouilla, Seuil, 1987
Rires d'homme entre deux pluies, Grasset, 1990
Le Bouquet des expressions imagées, with Sylvie Clava, Seuil, 1990
La Duchesse de Mali, Grasset, 1991
Marguerite devant les pourceaux, Grasset, 1991
Mots d'amour, Seuil, 1993
Bal à Koror, Grasset, 1994
Le Voyage de Karnantioul, Éditions du Laquet, 1997
Le Guide du français familier, Seuil, 1998
Histoire de la Chanson française, Volumes 1 and 2, Seuil, 1998
La Mort du français, Plon, 1999
Donadini, Séguier, 2001
Chansons sensuelles, Textuel, 2004
La puce à l'oreille, Denoël, 2005 (first published by Stock, 1978)
Loin des forêts rouges, Denoël, 2005
Au plaisir des jouets : 150 ans de catalogues, Hoëbeke, 2005
Fraises des bois, La Main parle, 2002
Au Plaisir des mots, éd. Balland, 2004 ;
Au Plaisir des mots : les meilleures chroniques, éd. Denoël, 2005
Loin des Forêts rouges : roman, éd. Denoël, 2005
Le Monument, Balland, 2005
Les Origimots, Gallimard Jeunesse, 2006
Pierrette qui roule ... Les terminaisons dangereuses, Mots et Cie, 2007
La Chienne de ma vie, Buchet Chastel, 2007
La Dame de l'argonaute, éd. Denoël, 2009

« Marcelle », text in *Inconnues Corréziennes, résonances d'écrivains*.
Ouvrage collectif, éd. Libel, 2009
Jojo l'animain : *conte jeunesse*, Tertium éditions, 2010
Petit dictionnaire du français familier, Points, 2012

Articles

« Discours aux nénuphars », *Revue Des Deux Mondes*, November 1991, pp
115-128
« L'Éloge de la dictée », *Défense de la langue française*, 18 November
2010

GENERAL BIBLIOGRAPHY

Place of publication is Paris, unless otherwise stated.

Académie française   1835 *Dictionnaire de l'Académie française*
Sixième édition
Firmin Didot Frères

_____   1932-1935 *Dictionnaire de l'Académie française* Huitième édition
Hachette

_____   1932 *Grammaire de l'Académie française*
Firmin-Didot

_____   1992 *Dictionnaire de l'Académie française*
Neuvième édition, Tome I, A-Enzyme
L'Imprimerie nationale

_____   1993 *Dictionnaire de l'Académie française*
*n*euvième édition, Tome II, Éocène-Étendue
Direction des Journaux officiels

Allais, Alphonse   1898 *Amours, Délices et Orgues*
Paul Ollendorff

Anglade, Joseph   1961 *Grammaire élémentaire de l'ancien français* Treizième Édition
Armand Colin

Anonymous   1593-4 *La Satyre ménippée*
Jamet Mettayer

_____ and Nithard   842 *Les Serments de Strasbourg*
L'Abbaye de Saint-Médard, Soissons

Barbusse, Henri   1924 *Carnets de guerre*
Éditions Douin

Barral, Marcel

1980 *L'imparfait du subjonctif*
A & Picard

Barthes, Roland

1966 *Critique et vérité*
Éditions du Seuil

Batchelor, Ronald E
& Offord, Malcolm H

1982 *A guide to contemporary French usage*
Cambridge University Press

Beauvais, Robert

1970 *L'Hexagonal tel qu'on le parle*
Hachette

_____

1975 *Le français kiskose*
Fayard

Bénac, Henri

1956 *Dictionnaire des synonymes*
Librairie Hachette

Benjamin, René

1918 *Les Rapatriés*
Berger-Levrault

Béronie, Nicolas
& Vialle, Joseph-Anne

nd *Dictionnaire du patois du Bas-Limousin (Corrèze)*
M Drappeau, Tulle

Bled, Édouard & Odette

1954 *Cours supérieur d'orthographe*
Classiques Hachette

Bottequin, Armand

1945 *Difficultés et finesses de langage*
Éditions Daphné, Ghent

Bourgeade, Pierre

1991 *Chroniques du français quotidien*
Belfond

Bouvier, Jean-Claude

2007 *Les noms de rues disent la ville*
Éditions Christine Bonneton

Brewer, E C
(Revised by Evans, I H)

1974 *Dictionary of Phrase and Fable*
Cassell, London

de Broglie, Gabriel	1986 *Le français, pour qu'il vive* Gallimard
Bruneau, Charles	1955 *Petite histoire de la langue française* Armand Colin
Brunot, Ferdinand	1932 *Observations sur la Grammaire de l'Académie française* Droz, Geneva
_____	1936 *La pensée et la langue* 3e édition Masson
Burney, Pierre	1967 *L'Orthographe* Presses universitaires de France
Camus, Albert	1942 *L'Étranger* Gallimard
_____	1947 *La Peste* Gallimard
Capelovici, Jacques	1988 « Le massacre de l'orthographe » *Le Figaro,* 22 mai, p 2
_____	1990 *Le français sans fautes* Acropole
_____	1992 *Guide du français correct* Archipel
Catach, Nina	1989 *Les délires de l'orthographe* Plon
Cellard, Jacques	1983 'Les chroniques de langage' *La norme linguistique,* Bédard & Maurais Le Robert
_____	1985 *Histoires de mots* Éditions La Découverte/Le Monde

Cellard, Jacques

1986a *Histoires de mots II*
Éditions La Découverte/Le Monde

—————

1986b *Les racines latines du vocabulaire français*
Duculot, Paris/Gembloux

Chapelan, Maurice
(writing as Aristide)

1989 *La langue française dans tous ses débats*
Bourin

Choux, Jules

1869 *Le petit citateur*
Paphos, Brussels

Conseil Supérieur
de la Langue française

1990 *Les Rectifications de l'Orthographe*
(Journal Officiel de la République française n°
100, 6 December 1990)
Direction des Journaux officiels

Couté, Gaston

1976-1977 *La chanson d'un gars qu'a mal tourné, œuvres complètes en cinq volumes*
Éditions Le vent du ch'min, Saint-Denis

Dauzat, Albert

1953 *Le français moderne* volume 21
Éditions d'Artrey

—————

1954 *Le guide du bon usage*
Delagrave

Défense de la langue
française

1992 *40 ans de Défense de la langue française*
Délégation Générale à la Langue française

Délégation générale
à la langue française

1993 *Dictionnaire des termes officiels*
8e édition
Direction des Journaux officiels

Delvau, Alfred

1867 *Dictionnaire de la langue verte*
Édouard Dentu

Deniau, Xavier

1983 *La Francophonie*
Presses Universitaires Françaises

Depardon, Raymond

2006 *La ferme du Garet*
Actes Sud, Arles

Deronne, Emmanuel

2012 in *Argotica* Nº 1 « Hommage à Claude Duneton (1935-2012) »
University of Craiova, Romania

Désirat, Claude & Hordé, Tristan

1976 *La langue française au 20ᵉ siècle*
Bordas

Desonay, Fernand et al.

1966 *Mélanges de grammaire française offerts à M Maurice Grevisse*
Duculot, Gembloux

Didot, Ambroise Firmin

1868 *Observations sur l'orthographe (ou ortografie) française*
Ambroise Firmin Didot

[Dossiers du Canard]

1989 *La tournée des pages*
Les Dossiers du Canard

_____

1993 *Made in France*
Les Dossiers du Canard

Dournon, Jean-Yves

1982 *Le Grand Dictionnaire des Citations françaises*
Acropole

Du Bellay, Joachim

1972 *Défense et Illustration de la Langue française* (1549)
Bordas

Duez, Nathanaël

1659 *Dittionario italiano e francese*
Jean Elsevier, Leiden

Dupas, Alain & Frèches, José

1987 *Modernissimots*
J C Lattès

Dupré, Paul

1969 *Encyclopédie des Citations*
Éditions de Trévise

Dupré, Paul

1972 *Encyclopédie du bon français* (3 vols)
Éditions de Trévise

Dutourd, Jean

1963 *Rivarol : Les plus belles pages*
Mercure de France

—————

1986a 'S.O.S. Langue française' *Figaro
Magazine,* 11 janvier : 11-17
Le Figaro

Esnault, Gaston

1919 *Le poilu tel qu'il se parle*
Bossard

—————

1965 *Dictionnaire historique des argots français*
Larousse

Estienne, Robert

1539-1549 *Dictionnaire français-latin*
Éditions Robert Estienne

Fombeure, Maurice

1948 *Les godillots sont lourds*
Gallimard

Francard, Michel, et al.

2010 *Dictionnaire des belgicismes*
Duculot (Paris-Louvain-la-Neuve)

France, Hector

1907 *Dictionnaire de la langue verte
(Appendice)*
Librairie du Progrès

François, Frédéric et al.

1983 *J'cause français, non ?...*
La Découverte/Maspero (APREF)

Franlain

1990 *100 dictées pièges*
Marabout, Alleur (Belgium)

Furetière, Antoine
Rey, Alain (Éd.)

1978 *Dictionnaire Universel* (1690)
Le Robert

[Furetière et] les Jésuites

1771 *Dictionnaire de Trévoux*
Compagnie des libraires associés

Gay, Sophie	1837 *Salons célèbres* Dumont
Genlis, Madame la Comtesse de	1823 *Les Veillées de la chaumière* Lecointe et Durey
Gide, André	1946 *Journal :* 1939-1942 La Pléiade
————	1951 *Journal :* 1889-1939 Gallimard
Girodet, Jean	1986 *Pièges et difficultés de la langue française* Bordas
Goosse, André	1991 *La « nouvelle » orthographe* Duculot, Paris-Louvain
Grevisse, Maurice	1962 *Problèmes de langage* Presses Universitaires Françaises
————	1963 *Problèmes de langage,* deuxième série Presses Universitaires Françaises
————	1964 *Problèmes de langage,* troisième série Presses Universitaires Françaises
————	1969 *Problèmes de langage,* quatrième série Duculot, Gembloux
————	1970 *Problèmes de langage,* cinquième série Duculot, Gembloux
————	1973 *Le français correct* Duculot (Paris-Gembloux)
————	1975 *Le participe passé* Duculot (Paris-Gembloux)

Grevisse, Maurice — 1980 *Le Bon Usage,* 11ᵉ édition
Duculot (Paris-Gembloux)

_____ — 1986 *Le Bon Usage,* 12ᵉ édition
Duculot (Paris-Gembloux)

_____ — 1990 *Précis de grammaire française*
2ᵉ édition
Duculot (Paris - Louvain-la-Neuve)

_____ — 2016 *Le Bon Usage*
Duculot (Paris-Louvain-la-Neuve)

_____ & Lenoble-Pinson, Michèle — 2010 *Le Français correct, guide pratique des difficultés*
De Boeck-Duculot

Groult, Benoîte — 1984 'Je suis une écrivaine' *Médias et Langage* M-1997-19/20 : 20-25

Hagège, Claude — 1985 *L'homme de paroles* (2ᵉ édition)
Fayard

_____ — 1987 *Le français et les siècles*
Éditions Odile Jacob

_____ — 1992 *Le souffle de la langue*
Éditions Odile Jacob

_____ — 2009 *Dictionnaire amoureux des langues*
Plon

Hanse, Joseph — 1949 *Dictionnaire des difficultés grammaticales et lexicologiques*
Baude, Brussels

Hanse, Joseph — 1983 *Nouveau dictionnaire des difficultés du français moderne*
Duculot, Gembloux

Harmer, Lewis Charles   1979 *Uncertainties in French Grammar*
                           Cambridge University Press

Hatin, Eugène   1965 *Bibliographie historique et critique de
                           la presse périodique française*
                           Georg Olms, Hildesheim

Hatzfeld, Adolphe et al.   1926 *Dictionnaire général de la langue
                           française*
                           Delagrave

Haut Comité de la   *1975 La Loi relative à l'emploi de la
langue française   langue française*
                           La Documentation française

Hégo, Jean-Marie   1989 'Les tentatives de réforme' *Le livre de
                           l'orthographe* (ed. by Bernard Pivot, pp 21-31)
                           Hatier

Jouette, André   1992 *Les pièges du français actuel*
                           Marabout, Alleur, Belgium
_____   1995 *Dictionnaire d'orthographe*
                           Le Robert

Lacroix, Grégoire   2009 *Les Nouveaux Euphorismes de Grégoire*
                           Éditions Max Milo

[Lafitte]   1984 *Who's Who in France 1984-85*
                           Lafitte

La Fontaine, Jean de   1668-1694 *Les Fables*
                           D Thierry ; C Barbin

Lair, Mathias   1990 *Les bras m'en tombent*
                           Acropole

Landais, Napoléon   1836 *Dictionnaire Général et Grammatical
                           des dictionnaires français*
                           Bureau Central Des Dictionnaires

Lorédan Larchey, Étienne   1862 *Les Excentricités du langage*
Édouard Dentu

[Larousse]   1964 *Grammaire du français contemporain*
Librairie Larousse

————   1971 *Dictionnaire du français contemporain*
Librairie Larousse

————   1994 *Petit Larousse*
Librairie Larousse

Laurent, Jacques   1988 *Le français en cage*
Grasset

Le Bidois, Georges   1967-8 *Syntaxe du français moderne* 2e édition
& Robert   Picard

Le Bidois, Robert   1970 *Les mots trompeurs*
Hachette

Le Gal, Étienne   1928 *Ne dites pas ... mais dites*
Delagrave

————   1953 *Parlons mieux*
Delagrave

————   1961 *Le parler vivant au XXe siècle*
Denoël

Léon, Pierre R   1966 *Prononciation du français standard*
Didier

Le Roux, Philibert J   1750 (1ère éd 1718) *Le Dictionnaire comique*
Michel Charles Le Cène, Amsterdam

Littré, Émile   1863 *Dictionnaire de la langue française*
Hachette

————   1873 *Dictionnaire de la langue française*
Hachette

Littré, Émile	1960 *Dictionnaire de la Langue française* Gallimard-Hachette
Mamavi, Gina & Depecker, Loïc	1992 *Logiciel et épinglette* Délégation de la langue française
Mamavi, Gina	1993 'Terminologie' *Les Brèves* 2ᵉ trimestre 1993, I-IV Délégation générale à la langue française
_____ & Depecker, Loïc	1993 'Commissions ministérielles de Terminologie' *Les Brèves* 1ᵉʳ trimestre 1993 p 3 Délégation générale à la langue française
Marks, Georgette A & Johnson, Charles B	1984 Harrap's *Slang Dictionary* Harrap, London
Martinet, André	1969 *Le français sans fard* Presses Universitaires de France
Martinet, André & Walter, Henriette	1973 *Dictionnaire de la Prononciation française dans son usage réel* France-Expansion
Mercier, Louis-Sébastien	1771 *L'An 2440, rêve s'il en fut jamais* Van-Harrevelt, Amsterdam
Merle, Pierre	1989 *Dictionnaire du français branché* & *Guide du français tic et toc* Éditions du Seuil
_____	2007 *Le Français mal-t-à-propos* L'Archipel
_____	2008 *De nos tics de langage* Éditions Fetjaine
Meung, Jean de	ca 1275 *Le Roman de la rose* Félix Lecoy (1965)

Meunier, Claude 2010 *Petit Abécédaire du rire*
Seuil

Mots-Clés 2017 *L'écriture inclusive*
Mots-Clés

Munro-Hill, Mary 1986 "Aristide of *Le Figaro*" MA Thesis
University of Hull, UK

———— 1994 "Aristide and the chroniques du langage
in the French Press" PhD Thesis
University of Hull, UK

———— 2017 *Aristide of Le Figaro*
Cambridge Scholars Publishing, Newcastle

Nicot, Jean 1606 *Trésor de la langue française*
David Douceur

Noreiko, Stephen 1985 *A la tienne ... French Word Games*
Lochee Publications, Dundee

Offord, Malcolm 1990 *Varieties of Contemporary French*
Macmillan

Orwell, George 1946 *Politics and the English Language*
Horizon, London

Partington, Angela 1992 *The Oxford Dictionary of Quotations*
BCA, London

Pennebaker, James & 2010 Article in *Journal of Personality and*
Ireland, Molly *Social Psychology*
University of Texas

Pivot, Bernard 1968 *Les critiques littéraires*
Flammarion

———— 1989 *Le livre de l'orthographe*
Hatier

Pope, Mildred Katharine — 1952 *From Latin to Modern French* 2nd Edition
Manchester University Press

Quemada, Bernard — 1970 *Bibliographie des chroniques de langage tome I (1950-1965)*
Centre d'étude du français moderne et contemporain (Éd B Quemada)

———— 1971 *Trésor de la langue française*
Éditions du Centre national de la Recherche scientifique (Éd B Quemada)

———— 1972 *Bibliographie des chroniques de langage* tome II (1966-1970)
Centre d'étude du français moderne et contemporain (Éd B Quemada)
Didier

Rey, Alain — 2014 « L'orthographe est un marqueur social ; elle donne une image de soi », *20 Minutes,* 4 September

Rey-Debove, Josette & Le Beau-Bensa, Béatrice — 1991 *La Réforme de l'orthographe au banc d'essai du Robert*
Dictionnaires Le Robert

Richelet, Pierre — 1680 *Dictionnaire français*
Jean Herman Widerhold, Geneva

———— 1694 *Dictionnaire français*
Gaillard, Cologne

Rivarol, Antoine de — [1784] *Discours sur l'Universalité de la Langue française*
Éd M Hervier, 1921
Delagrave

———— [1784] *Discours sur l'Universalité de la Langue française* Éd T Suran, 1930
Didier

Rivarol, Antoine de   [1784] *Discours sur l'Universalité de la
                             Langue française* Éd M Favergeat, 1936
                             Larousse

Robert, Paul   1957 *Dictionnaire alphabétique et analogique
                             de la Langue française*
                             Société du Nouveau Littré

————————   1965 *Aventures et mésaventures d'un
                             dictionnaire*
                             Société du nouveau Littré « Le Robert »

————————   1966 *Le Grand Robert*
                             Société du Nouveau Littré

Rudder, Orlando de   1986 *Le français qui se cause*
                             Balland

Saint-Ange, E   1927 *La bonne cuisine*
                             Larousse

Saint Robert,   1986 *Lettre ouverte à ceux qui en perdent
Philippe de   leur français*
                             Albin Michel

Sauvageot, Aurélien   1962 *Français écrit, français parlé*
                             Larousse

————————   1964 *Portrait du vocabulaire français*
                             Larousse

Taillandier, François   2009 *La Langue française au défi*
                             Flammarion

Thérive, André   1940 *Querelles de langage*
                             Stock

————————   1954 *Libre histoire de la langue française*
                             Stock

Thérive, André   1956 *Clinique du langage*
                                  Grasset

―――――   1962 *Procès de langage*
                                  Stock

Thévenot, Jean   1976 *He ! la France, ton français fout le camp !*
                                  Duculot, Gembloux

Thimonnier, René   1976 *Le système graphique du français*
                                  Plon

Thomas, Adolphe V   1956 *Dictionnaire des difficultés de la
                                  langue française*
                                  Larousse

Trailles, Paul & Henri de   1872 *Les Femmes de France pendant la guerre
                            de 1870*
                            François Polo

Treps, Marie   1997 *Le Dico des Mots-caresses*
                                  Éditions du Seuil

Vanneste, Alex   2005 *Le français du XXIe siècle : introduction
                                  à la francophonie, éléments de phonétique, de
                                  phonologie et de morphologie*
                                  Garant, Antwerp

Vaugelas, Claude   1970 *Remarques sur la langue française*
Favre de   Facsimilé de l'édition originale (1647)
                                  (Reprint of edition of Streicher, Droz, 1934)
                                  Slatkine, Geneva

Virmaître, Charles   1894 *Dictionnaire de l'argot fin-de-siècle*
                                  A Charles

Voltaire   1877-1885 *Œuvres complètes de Voltaire*
                                  éd. Louis Moland
                                  Garnier

138

General Bibliography

Wagner, Robert-Léon &
Pinchon, Jacqueline

1962 *Grammaire du français classique
et moderne*
Hachette

Walter, Henriette

1988 *Le français dans tous les sens*
Robert Laffont

Warnant, Léon

1962 *Dictionnaire de la prononciation
française*
Duculot, Gembloux

INDEX